Taxation: A Very Short Introduction

VERY SHORT INTRODUCTIONS are for anyone wanting a stimulating and accessible way into a new subject. They are written by experts, and have been translated into more than 40 different languages.

The series began in 1995, and now covers a wide variety of topics in every discipline. The VSI library now contains over 350 volumes—a Very Short Introduction to everything from Psychology and Philosophy of Science to American History and Relativity—and continues to grow in every subject area.

Very Short Introductions available now:

ACCOUNTING Christopher Nobes
ADVERTISING Winston Fletcher
AFRICAN AMERICAN
    RELIGION Eddie S. Glaude Jr.
AFRICAN HISTORY John Parker and
    Richard Rathbone
AFRICAN RELIGIONS Jacob K. Olupona
AGNOSTICISM Robin Le Poidevin
ALEXANDER THE GREAT
    Hugh Bowden
AMERICAN HISTORY Paul S. Boyer
AMERICAN IMMIGRATION
    David A. Gerber
AMERICAN LEGAL HISTORY
    G. Edward White
AMERICAN POLITICAL HISTORY
    Donald Critchlow
AMERICAN POLITICAL PARTIES
    AND ELECTIONS L. Sandy Maisel
AMERICAN POLITICS Richard M. Valelly
THE AMERICAN PRESIDENCY
    Charles O. Jones
AMERICAN SLAVERY
    Heather Andrea Williams
THE AMERICAN WEST Stephen Aron
AMERICAN WOMEN'S HISTORY
    Susan Ware
ANAESTHESIA Aidan O'Donnell
ANARCHISM Colin Ward
ANCIENT ASSYRIA Karen Radner
ANCIENT EGYPT Ian Shaw
ANCIENT EGYPTIAN ART AND
    ARCHITECTURE Christina Riggs
ANCIENT GREECE Paul Cartledge

THE ANCIENT NEAR EAST
    Amanda H. Podany
ANCIENT PHILOSOPHY Julia Annas
ANCIENT WARFARE Harry Sidebottom
ANGELS David Albert Jones
ANGLICANISM Mark Chapman
THE ANGLO-SAXON AGE John Blair
THE ANIMAL KINGDOM
    Peter Holland
ANIMAL RIGHTS David DeGrazia
THE ANTARCTIC Klaus Dodds
ANTISEMITISM Steven Beller
ANXIETY Daniel Freeman and
    Jason Freeman
THE APOCRYPHAL GOSPELS
    Paul Foster
ARCHAEOLOGY Paul Bahn
ARCHITECTURE Andrew Ballantyne
ARISTOCRACY William Doyle
ARISTOTLE Jonathan Barnes
ART HISTORY Dana Arnold
ART THEORY Cynthia Freeland
ASTROBIOLOGY David C. Catling
ATHEISM Julian Baggini
AUGUSTINE Henry Chadwick
AUSTRALIA Kenneth Morgan
AUTISM Uta Frith
THE AVANT GARDE David Cottington
THE AZTECS David Carrasco
BACTERIA Sebastian G. B. Amyes
BARTHES Jonathan Culler
THE BEATS David Sterritt
BEAUTY Roger Scruton
BESTSELLERS John Sutherland

THE BIBLE John Riches
BIBLICAL ARCHAEOLOGY
    Eric H. Cline
BIOGRAPHY Hermione Lee
THE BLUES Elijah Wald
THE BOOK OF MORMON
    Terryl Givens
BORDERS Alexander C. Diener and
    Joshua Hagen
THE BRAIN Michael O'Shea
THE BRITISH CONSTITUTION
    Martin Loughlin
THE BRITISH EMPIRE Ashley Jackson
BRITISH POLITICS Anthony Wright
BUDDHA Michael Carrithers
BUDDHISM Damien Keown
BUDDHIST ETHICS Damien Keown
CANCER Nicholas James
CAPITALISM James Fulcher
CATHOLICISM Gerald O'Collins
CAUSATION Stephen Mumford and
    Rani Lill Anjum
THE CELL Terence Allen and
    Graham Cowling
THE CELTS Barry Cunliffe
CHAOS Leonard Smith
CHEMISTRY Peter Atkins
CHILD PSYCHOLOGY Usha Goswami
CHILDREN'S LITERATURE
    Kimberley Reynolds
CHINESE LITERATURE Sabina Knight
CHOICE THEORY Michael Allingham
CHRISTIAN ART Beth Williamson
CHRISTIAN ETHICS D. Stephen Long
CHRISTIANITY Linda Woodhead
CITIZENSHIP Richard Bellamy
CIVIL ENGINEERING David Muir Wood
CLASSICAL LITERATURE William Allan
CLASSICAL MYTHOLOGY
    Helen Morales
CLASSICS Mary Beard and John Henderson
CLAUSEWITZ Michael Howard
CLIMATE Mark Maslin
THE COLD WAR Robert McMahon
COLONIAL AMERICA Alan Taylor
COLONIAL LATIN AMERICAN
    LITERATURE Rolena Adorno
COMEDY Matthew Bevis
COMMUNISM Leslie Holmes
COMPLEXITY John H. Holland

THE COMPUTER Darrel Ince
CONFUCIANISM Daniel K. Gardner
THE CONQUISTADORS
    Matthew Restall and
    Felipe Fernández-Armesto
CONSCIENCE Paul Strohm
CONSCIOUSNESS Susan Blackmore
CONTEMPORARY ART Julian Stallabrass
CONTEMPORARY FICTION
    Robert Eaglestone
CONTINENTAL PHILOSOPHY
    Simon Critchley
CORAL REEFS Charles Sheppard
CORPORATE SOCIAL RESPONSIBILITY
    Jeremy Moon
CORRUPTION Leslie Holmes
COSMOLOGY Peter Coles
CRITICAL THEORY Stephen Eric Bronner
THE CRUSADES Christopher Tyerman
CRYPTOGRAPHY Fred Piper and
    Sean Murphy
THE CULTURAL REVOLUTION
    Richard Curt Kraus
DADA AND SURREALISM
    David Hopkins
DANTE Peter Hainsworth and David Robey
DARWIN Jonathan Howard
THE DEAD SEA SCROLLS Timothy Lim
DEMOCRACY Bernard Crick
DERRIDA Simon Glendinning
DESCARTES Tom Sorell
DESERTS Nick Middleton
DESIGN John Heskett
DEVELOPMENTAL BIOLOGY
    Lewis Wolpert
THE DEVIL Darren Oldridge
DIASPORA Kevin Kenny
DICTIONARIES Lynda Mugglestone
DINOSAURS David Norman
DIPLOMACY Joseph M. Siracusa
DOCUMENTARY FILM
    Patricia Aufderheide
DREAMING J. Allan Hobson
DRUGS Leslie Iversen
DRUIDS Barry Cunliffe
EARLY MUSIC Thomas Forrest Kelly
THE EARTH Martin Redfern
ECONOMICS Partha Dasgupta
EDUCATION Gary Thomas
EGYPTIAN MYTH Geraldine Pinch

EIGHTEENTH-CENTURY BRITAIN
    Paul Langford
THE ELEMENTS Philip Ball
EMOTION Dylan Evans
EMPIRE Stephen Howe
ENGELS Terrell Carver
ENGINEERING David Blockley
ENGLISH LITERATURE Jonathan Bate
ENTREPRENEURSHIP Paul Westhead
    and Mike Wright
ENVIRONMENTAL
    ECONOMICS Stephen Smith
EPIDEMIOLOGY Rodolfo Saracci
ETHICS Simon Blackburn
ETHNOMUSICOLOGY Timothy Rice
THE ETRUSCANS Christopher Smith
THE EUROPEAN UNION John Pinder
    and Simon Usherwood
EVOLUTION Brian and
    Deborah Charlesworth
EXISTENTIALISM Thomas Flynn
EXPLORATION Stewart A. Weaver
THE EYE Michael Land
FAMILY LAW Jonathan Herring
FASCISM Kevin Passmore
FASHION Rebecca Arnold
FEMINISM Margaret Walters
FILM Michael Wood
FILM MUSIC Kathryn Kalinak
THE FIRST WORLD WAR
    Michael Howard
FOLK MUSIC Mark Slobin
FOOD John Krebs
FORENSIC PSYCHOLOGY David Canter
FORENSIC SCIENCE Jim Fraser
FOSSILS Keith Thomson
FOUCAULT Gary Gutting
FRACTALS Kenneth Falconer
FREE SPEECH Nigel Warburton
FREE WILL Thomas Pink
FRENCH LITERATURE John D. Lyons
THE FRENCH REVOLUTION
    William Doyle
FREUD Anthony Storr
FUNDAMENTALISM Malise Ruthven
GALAXIES John Gribbin
GALILEO Stillman Drake
GAME THEORY Ken Binmore
GANDHI Bhikhu Parekh
GENES Jonathan Slack

GENIUS Andrew Robinson
GEOGRAPHY John Matthews and
    David Herbert
GEOPOLITICS Klaus Dodds
GERMAN LITERATURE Nicholas Boyle
GERMAN PHILOSOPHY Andrew Bowie
GLOBAL CATASTROPHES Bill McGuire
GLOBAL ECONOMIC HISTORY
    Robert C. Allen
GLOBALIZATION Manfred Steger
GOD John Bowker
THE GOTHIC Nick Groom
GOVERNANCE Mark Bevir
THE GREAT DEPRESSION AND THE
    NEW DEAL Eric Rauchway
HABERMAS James Gordon Finlayson
HAPPINESS Daniel M. Haybron
HEGEL Peter Singer
HEIDEGGER Michael Inwood
HERODOTUS Jennifer T. Roberts
HIEROGLYPHS Penelope Wilson
HINDUISM Kim Knott
HISTORY John H. Arnold
THE HISTORY OF ASTRONOMY
    Michael Hoskin
THE HISTORY OF LIFE Michael Benton
THE HISTORY OF MATHEMATICS
    Jacqueline Stedall
THE HISTORY OF MEDICINE
    William Bynum
THE HISTORY OF TIME
    Leofranc Holford-Strevens
HIV/AIDS Alan Whiteside
HOBBES Richard Tuck
HORMONES Martin Luck
HUMAN ANATOMY Leslie Klenerman
HUMAN EVOLUTION Bernard Wood
HUMAN RIGHTS Andrew Clapham
HUMANISM Stephen Law
HUME A. J. Ayer
HUMOUR Noël Carroll
THE ICE AGE Jamie Woodward
IDEOLOGY Michael Freeden
INDIAN PHILOSOPHY Sue Hamilton
INFORMATION Luciano Floridi
INNOVATION Mark Dodgson and
    David Gann
INTELLIGENCE Ian J. Deary
INTERNATIONAL MIGRATION
    Khalid Koser

INTERNATIONAL RELATIONS
  Paul Wilkinson
INTERNATIONAL SECURITY
  Christopher S. Browning
IRAN Ali M. Ansari
ISLAM Malise Ruthven
ISLAMIC HISTORY Adam Silverstein
ITALIAN LITERATURE
  Peter Hainsworth and David Robey
JESUS Richard Bauckham
JOURNALISM Ian Hargreaves
JUDAISM Norman Solomon
JUNG Anthony Stevens
KABBALAH Joseph Dan
KAFKA Ritchie Robertson
KANT Roger Scruton
KEYNES Robert Skidelsky
KIERKEGAARD Patrick Gardiner
KNOWLEDGE Jennifer Nagel
THE KORAN Michael Cook
LANDSCAPE ARCHITECTURE
  Ian H. Thompson
LANDSCAPES AND
  GEOMORPHOLOGY
  Andrew Goudie and Heather Viles
LANGUAGES Stephen R. Anderson
LATE ANTIQUITY Gillian Clark
LAW Raymond Wacks
THE LAWS OF THERMODYNAMICS
  Peter Atkins
LEADERSHIP Keith Grint
LINCOLN Allen C. Guelzo
LINGUISTICS Peter Matthews
LITERARY THEORY Jonathan Culler
LOCKE John Dunn
LOGIC Graham Priest
LOVE Ronald de Sousa
MACHIAVELLI Quentin Skinner
MADNESS Andrew Scull
MAGIC Owen Davies
MAGNA CARTA Nicholas Vincent
MAGNETISM Stephen Blundell
MALTHUS Donald Winch
MANAGEMENT John Hendry
MAO Delia Davin
MARINE BIOLOGY Philip V. Mladenov
THE MARQUIS DE SADE John Phillips
MARTIN LUTHER Scott H. Hendrix
MARTYRDOM Jolyon Mitchell
MARX Peter Singer

MATERIALS Christopher Hall
MATHEMATICS Timothy Gowers
THE MEANING OF LIFE
  Terry Eagleton
MEDICAL ETHICS Tony Hope
MEDICAL LAW Charles Foster
MEDIEVAL BRITAIN John Gillingham
  and Ralph A. Griffiths
MEMORY Jonathan K. Foster
METAPHYSICS Stephen Mumford
MICHAEL FARADAY
  Frank A. J. L. James
MICROBIOLOGY Nicholas P. Money
MICROECONOMICS Avinash Dixit
THE MIDDLE AGES Miri Rubin
MINERALS David Vaughan
MODERN ART David Cottington
MODERN CHINA Rana Mitter
MODERN FRANCE
  Vanessa R. Schwartz
MODERN IRELAND Senia Pašeta
MODERN JAPAN
  Christopher Goto-Jones
MODERN LATIN AMERICAN
  LITERATURE
  Roberto González Echevarría
MODERN WAR Richard English
MODERNISM Christopher Butler
MOLECULES Philip Ball
THE MONGOLS Morris Rossabi
MORMONISM
  Richard Lyman Bushman
MUHAMMAD Jonathan A. C. Brown
MULTICULTURALISM Ali Rattansi
MUSIC Nicholas Cook
MYTH Robert A. Segal
THE NAPOLEONIC WARS
  Mike Rapport
NATIONALISM Steven Grosby
NELSON MANDELA Elleke Boehmer
NEOLIBERALISM Manfred Steger and
  Ravi Roy
NETWORKS Guido Caldarelli and
  Michele Catanzaro
THE NEW TESTAMENT
  Luke Timothy Johnson
THE NEW TESTAMENT AS
  LITERATURE Kyle Keefer
NEWTON Robert Iliffe
NIETZSCHE Michael Tanner

NINETEENTH-CENTURY
    BRITAIN Christopher Harvie and
    H. C. G. Matthew
THE NORMAN CONQUEST
    George Garnett
NORTH AMERICAN INDIANS
    Theda Perdue and Michael D. Green
NORTHERN IRELAND Marc Mulholland
NOTHING Frank Close
NUCLEAR POWER Maxwell Irvine
NUCLEAR WEAPONS
    Joseph M. Siracusa
NUMBERS Peter M. Higgins
NUTRITION David A. Bender
OBJECTIVITY Stephen Gaukroger
THE OLD TESTAMENT
    Michael D. Coogan
THE ORCHESTRA D. Kern Holoman
ORGANIZATIONS Mary Jo Hatch
PAGANISM Owen Davies
THE PALESTINIAN-ISRAELI
    CONFLICT Martin Bunton
PARTICLE PHYSICS Frank Close
PAUL E. P. Sanders
PEACE Oliver P. Richmond
PENTECOSTALISM William K. Kay
THE PERIODIC TABLE Eric R. Scerri
PHILOSOPHY Edward Craig
PHILOSOPHY OF LAW
    Raymond Wacks
PHILOSOPHY OF SCIENCE
    Samir Okasha
PHOTOGRAPHY Steve Edwards
PHYSICAL CHEMISTRY Peter Atkins
PILGRIMAGE Ian Reader
PLAGUE Paul Slack
PLANETS David A. Rothery
PLANTS Timothy Walker
PLATE TECTONICS Peter Molnar
PLATO Julia Annas
POLITICAL PHILOSOPHY
    David Miller
POLITICS Kenneth Minogue
POSTCOLONIALISM Robert Young
POSTMODERNISM Christopher Butler
POSTSTRUCTURALISM
    Catherine Belsey
PREHISTORY Chris Gosden
PRESOCRATIC PHILOSOPHY
    Catherine Osborne

PRIVACY Raymond Wacks
PROBABILITY John Haigh
PROGRESSIVISM Walter Nugent
PROTESTANTISM Mark A. Noll
PSYCHIATRY Tom Burns
PSYCHOLOGY Gillian Butler and
    Freda McManus
PSYCHOTHERAPY Tom Burns and
    Eva Burns-Lundgren
PURITANISM Francis J. Bremer
THE QUAKERS Pink Dandelion
QUANTUM THEORY John Polkinghorne
RACISM Ali Rattansi
RADIOACTIVITY Claudio Tuniz
RASTAFARI Ennis B. Edmonds
THE REAGAN REVOLUTION Gil Troy
REALITY Jan Westerhoff
THE REFORMATION Peter Marshall
RELATIVITY Russell Stannard
RELIGION IN AMERICA Timothy Beal
THE RENAISSANCE Jerry Brotton
RENAISSANCE ART
    Geraldine A. Johnson
REVOLUTIONS Jack A. Goldstone
RHETORIC Richard Toye
RISK Baruch Fischhoff and John Kadvany
RITUAL Barry Stephenson
RIVERS Nick Middleton
ROBOTICS Alan Winfield
ROMAN BRITAIN Peter Salway
THE ROMAN EMPIRE
    Christopher Kelly
THE ROMAN REPUBLIC
    David M. Gwynn
ROMANTICISM Michael Ferber
ROUSSEAU Robert Wokler
RUSSELL A. C. Grayling
RUSSIAN HISTORY Geoffrey Hosking
RUSSIAN LITERATURE Catriona Kelly
THE RUSSIAN REVOLUTION
    S. A. Smith
SCHIZOPHRENIA Chris Frith and
    Eve Johnstone
SCHOPENHAUER
    Christopher Janaway
SCIENCE AND RELIGION
    Thomas Dixon
SCIENCE FICTION David Seed
THE SCIENTIFIC REVOLUTION
    Lawrence M. Principe

SCOTLAND Rab Houston
SEXUALITY Véronique Mottier
SHAKESPEARE Germaine Greer
SIKHISM Eleanor Nesbitt
THE SILK ROAD James A. Millward
SLEEP Steven W. Lockley and
    Russell G. Foster
SOCIAL AND CULTURAL
    ANTHROPOLOGY
    John Monaghan and Peter Just
SOCIALISM Michael Newman
SOCIOLINGUISTICS John Edwards
SOCIOLOGY Steve Bruce
SOCRATES C. C. W. Taylor
THE SOVIET UNION Stephen Lovell
THE SPANISH CIVIL WAR
    Helen Graham
SPANISH LITERATURE Jo Labanyi
SPINOZA Roger Scruton
SPIRITUALITY Philip Sheldrake
SPORT Mike Cronin
STARS Andrew King
STATISTICS David J. Hand
STEM CELLS Jonathan Slack
STRUCTURAL ENGINEERING
    David Blockley
STUART BRITAIN John Morrill
SUPERCONDUCTIVITY
    Stephen Blundell
SYMMETRY Ian Stewart
TAXATION Stephen Smith
TEETH Peter S. Ungar

TERRORISM Charles Townshend
THEATRE Marvin Carlson
THEOLOGY David F. Ford
THOMAS AQUINAS Fergus Kerr
THOUGHT Tim Bayne
TIBETAN BUDDHISM
    Matthew T. Kapstein
TOCQUEVILLE Harvey C. Mansfield
TRAGEDY Adrian Poole
THE TROJAN WAR Eric H. Cline
TRUST Katherine Hawley
THE TUDORS John Guy
TWENTIETH-CENTURY BRITAIN
    Kenneth O. Morgan
THE UNITED NATIONS
    Jussi M. Hanhimäki
THE U.S. CONGRESS
    Donald A. Ritchie
THE U.S. SUPREME COURT
    Linda Greenhouse
UTOPIANISM Lyman Tower Sargent
THE VIKINGS Julian Richards
VIRUSES Dorothy H. Crawford
WITCHCRAFT Malcolm Gaskill
WITTGENSTEIN A. C. Grayling
WORK Stephen Fineman
WORLD MUSIC Philip Bohlman
THE WORLD TRADE ORGANIZATION
    Amrita Narlikar
WORLD WAR II Gerhard L. Weinberg
WRITING AND SCRIPT
    Andrew Robinson

Available soon:

MICROSCOPY Terence Allen
LIBERALISM Michael Freeden
CRIME FICTION Richard Bradford

SOCIAL WORK Sally Holland and
    Jonathan Scourfield
FORESTS Jaboury Ghazoul

For more information visit our website

www.oup.com/vsi/

Stephen Smith

TAXATION

A Very Short Introduction

OXFORD
UNIVERSITY PRESS

OXFORD
UNIVERSITY PRESS

Great Clarendon Street, Oxford, OX2 6DP,
United Kingdom

Oxford University Press is a department of the University of Oxford.
It furthers the University's objective of excellence in research, scholarship,
and education by publishing worldwide. Oxford is a registered trade mark of
Oxford University Press in the UK and in certain other countries

First edition published in 2015

Impression: 6

Published in the United States of America by Oxford University Press
198 Madison Avenue, New York, NY 10016, United States of America

British Library Cataloguing in Publication Data
Data available

Library of Congress Control Number: 2014955268

ISBN 978-0-19-968369-7

Printed and bound by CPI Group (UK) Ltd, Croydon, CR0 4YY

Contents

Acknowledgements xiii

List of illustrations xv

Introduction 1

1 Why do we have taxes? 3

2 The structure of taxation 12

3 Who bears the tax burden? 31

4 Taxation and the economy 48

5 Tax evasion and enforcement 75

6 Issues in tax policy 97

Glossary 123

Further reading 125

Index 128

Acknowledgements

Many intellectual debts are owed when writing a book like this. First and foremost I would like to acknowledge how much I owe to my former colleagues at the Institute for Fiscal Studies (IFS), and in particular to John Kay who was Director of IFS when I joined the staff in 1985. For an economist interested in policy there can be few more stimulating places to work, where serious thinking about policy is informed by such a wealth of research, data, and evidence.

I have in particular benefited from the Mirrlees Review, a fundamental assessment of the UK tax system initiated by the IFS, which involved many of the world's leading academic researchers and tax policy thinkers. The reports published as a result of this work—the background papers in *Dimensions of Tax Design* and the final report of the Mirrlees review team *Tax by Design*, published in 2011—provide a remarkable synthesis of economic theory and evidence, and an authoritative manual for tax policy.

I have written this book during a period of sabbatical leave at Sciences Po in Paris. I am grateful to my own institution, UCL, for supporting this period of leave, and to the Economics Department at Sciences Po for providing me with such a congenial base for research and writing.

Finally, I would like to thank my editors at OUP, Andrea Keegan, Emma Ma, and Jenny Nugee, for their support and advice.

List of illustrations

1 Gallo-Roman relief from the 1st century CE showing taxes being paid **7**

Relief portraying paying of taxes, from Saintes (France)/ De Agostini Picture Library/ Bridgeman Images

2 International comparison of the level of taxation, selected countries **9**

Created using OECD (2014) *Revenue Statistics 1965–2012*

3 The structure of taxation in OECD countries, 1965 and 2011 **13**

Created using data from OECD (2014) *Revenue Statistics 1965–2012*

4 The structure of taxation in selected countries, 2011 **16**

Created using data from OECD (2014) *Revenue Statistics 1965–2012*

5 Income taxpayers queuing, New York, 1915 **17**

© Bettmann/CORBIS

6 'Duty Paid' by Ralph Hedley (1848–1913) **27**

Duty Paid, 1896 (oil on canvas), Hedley, Ralph (1848–1913)/ Sunderland Museums & Winter Garden Collection, Tyne & Wear, UK/Tyne & Wear Archives & Museums/Bridgeman Images

7 Economic incidence of a sales tax **34**

© The Author

8 Who pays the taxes? **45**

Created using data underlying Figure 4.3 in *Tax by Design: the Mirrlees Review* (2011)

9 The distortionary costs of taxation **52**

An artisan and his family looking forward to seeing more of the Sun when the Window Tax, imposed in 1696, would be repealed in 1851. Cartoon by Richard Doyle from *Punch*, London, 1851./Universal History Archive/UIG/Bridgeman Images

10 Distortionary cost of a sales tax **53**

© The Author

11 Taxation without fairness **59**
© Reuters/CORBIS

12 The marginal tax wedge **70**
Created using data from OECD
(2011) *Taxation and Employment*,
Figures 1.9–1.11

13 US IRS staff processing
income tax returns **78**
© Roger Ressmeyer/CORBIS

14 'Cheating on tax if
you have the chance.
Do you think this is
justified?' **88**
Created using data from
Benno Torgler, 'Tax morale
in Asian countries', *Journal
of Asian Economics*, 15
(2004): 237–66, Tables 1
and A1

15 The economist Adam Smith
(1723–98) **100**
Portrait of Adam Smith (Kirkcaldy
1723; Edinburgh 1790), Scottish
philosopher and economist.
Engraving/De Agostini Picture
Library/Bridgeman Images

16 Who gains and who loses from
a flat-rate income tax? **111**
Created using data from Clemens
Fuest, Andreas Peichl, and Thilo
Schaefer, 'Is a flat tax feasible in a
grown-up democracy of Western
Europe? A simulation study for
Germany', *International Tax and
Public Finance*, 15 (2008), Table 5

17 Who gets the benefit if VAT is
not levied on food? **114**
OECD (2007), OECD Economic
Surveys: Mexico 2007, OECD
Publishing. <http://dx.doi.org/
10.1787/eco_surveys-mex-2007-en>

Introduction

Taxation is crucial to the functioning of the modern state. Tax revenues pay for public services—roads, the courts, defence, welfare assistance to the poor and elderly—and, in many countries, much of health care and education too. Among the industrialized (Organisation for Economic Co-operation and Development (OECD)) countries, taxes took a quarter of national income in the United States in 2012, and on average almost two-fifths of national income in the member states of the European Union.

Taxes affect individuals in many ways. Taxes paid on income and spending directly reduce taxpayers' disposable income; taxpayers face the hassle of tax returns and making payments; and they may be anxious about the possibility of investigation and enforcement action. People also adapt their activities in various ways to reduce the impact of taxation—putting money into tax-free savings accounts, for example, or making shopping trips to other countries where taxes are lower.

It is hardly surprising, then, that taxation is so central to politics and to public debate. Politicians make reckless campaign promises about taxation and—if elected—then have to live with the uncomfortable consequences. Businesses lobby for tax breaks that they claim will create jobs and prosperity. One of the distinguishing differences between politicians on the left and those on the right is often their attitude to taxation, and to particular individual taxes. Many right-wing politicians advocate tax cuts and have a preference for taxes on spending rather than income taxes; politicians on the left are often more concerned with maintaining public services than with cutting taxes, and highlight the impact of taxes on spending on household living costs.

The iniquities and absurdities of taxation are a staple of dinner-party and pub conversation, and there are probably very few members of the public who have not voiced an opinion at some time about taxation and tax policy. Indeed, there are times when taxation seems able to trigger broad-based protest on a scale prompted by few other causes. Notoriously, the independence of the USA began with protests about the taxes levied by Britain: the cause of independence was promoted with the slogan 'No taxation without representation' and the stakes raised by the violent action taken in the Boston Tea Party. In more recent times, in the UK, public resentment about taxation has twice sparked remarkable civil disruption—the riots in the UK in 1990 in protest at the introduction of a local government poll tax and, a decade later, the campaign of transport blockades by hauliers, farmers, and others angered by motor fuel taxation.

The theme of this *Very Short Introduction* is that public decisions about taxation can be improved by a better understanding of the role of taxation, and of the nature and effects of different taxes. Although tax policy will always be a highly political issue, taxes have real effects on citizens and the economy that tax policy-makers need to weigh up. A wider public appreciation of the constraints and trade-offs in tax policy-making may help to lead to greater rationality in tax policy, and ultimately to better public decisions.

Chapter 1
Why do we have taxes?

Revenues: the sinews of the state
Cicero

Taxation is a theme that crops up with surprising frequency in popular music. It rarely figures positively. In their 1966 song, 'Taxman', the Beatles sang of a world in which they felt taxed at every turn. In the very same year, the Beatles' contemporaries, the Kinks, had a hit single, 'Sunny Afternoon', in which the singer laments that the taxman has made him penniless; all that he has left is the consolation of a lazy afternoon in the summer sunshine.

Why taxes should figure so strongly in popular music is not clear. Maybe successful popular musicians spend their career writing songs about the things that are most immediate and vital in their lives. When they were young and poor it was love, angst, and, perhaps, drugs. Once they find themselves on the escalator of fame, wealth, and endless touring, it is the misery of life on the road, divorce, venal managers...and their tax bill.

Away from popular music, taxation appears to figure little in our written or visual culture. True, there are plenty of cartoons, many of them, like most of the pop music lyrics, with more venom than humour. The celebrated cartoonist H.M. Bateman, a tart observer of English society in the first half of the 20th century, spent much of his later years embroiled in bitter warfare with the Inland Revenue, and encapsulated his vitriol in some brilliant, scathing, cartoons. But taxes figure little in literature, and—cartoons apart—are barely to be seen in the visual arts.

This absence contrasts with the enormous role that taxes play in our lives, and in the organization of society. In the UK, as in most countries in western Europe, more than one pound in every three earned is taken in taxation. Our lives and our society are closely engaged in activities that depend on taxation—public safety, defence, the courts, roads, schools, health care—not to mention public funding for the arts and culture. Taxes are at one and the same time hugely prominent in public debate, in political controversy, in the conversations we have in pubs, with taxi drivers, and with colleagues and friends—yet they are curiously invisible too. It is as if we don't want to admit—or don't fully comprehend—the fundamental role that they play in our society, our lives, and our living standards.

What is taxation?

So, what are taxes? Yes, we know. They are the money that is taken from us by the government. But taxes differ from the money that we spend in other ways in two distinctive respects.

To attempt a formal definition, taxes are compulsory payments, exacted by the state, that do not confer any direct individual entitlement to specific goods or services in return.

The second part of this definition is crucial, distinguishing taxes from the prices, fees, or charges that could be levied on the sale of goods and services by the state or state enterprises. While these, too, can generate public revenue, the fact that something is supplied directly in return for the payment means that they can be voluntary. As with things bought from the private sector, people pay if they want to buy the good or service in question, and if they would

4

rather use their money for other purposes they can choose to do so. By contrast, taxation involves compulsion—which crucially distinguishes taxation from most other activities in modern democracies. The compulsory nature of taxation doubtless accounts for much public hostility.

A key characteristic of taxation in modern tax systems is that taxation is 'parametric': in other words, it is governed by legislation which defines in advance the basis of individual tax liability. Typically, such legislation will define the tax base—in other words, the aspects of economic activity on which the tax will be charged, such as income, spending, or the value of property—and will specify how an individual's tax liability will be calculated, in a clear and predictable way. This has not always been a characteristic of taxation. At many times in the past taxes have been levied which have been arbitrary, and not based on clear and stable principles. If undertaken once only, economic confiscation of this sort may cause little economic harm, apart from the loss that taxpayers suffer through the resources which are confiscated. But regular confiscation can exert a chilling effect on economic activity—once people begin to believe that there is little point in doing anything if the fruits of their enterprise will merely provoke further confiscation. And arbitrary taxation—taxation which is not precisely governed by a legal framework specifying how liability to tax should be calculated—can offer undesirable scope for corruption to take hold.

Taxation in history

Taxation is by no means a modern phenomenon. Taxes, it would seem, were present at the dawn of recorded history. Some of the earliest written documents in existence, cuneiform clay tablets from Sumeria in southern Mesopotamia (modern-day Iraq) dating from around 3300 BCE, take the form of tax records: lists of gold, animals, and slaves received by the temples which formed the core of social organization in the Sumerian city-states. The need to record tax payments was, perhaps, one of the earliest reasons to develop some form of written record-keeping—and so it might be argued that taxation played a part in the development of writing itself.

The earliest taxes, in Mesopotamia, ancient Egypt, and elsewhere, take the form of shares or tithes of crops or other items of production, and also obligations to provide labour services, in the form of military service or work on construction projects. Money—currency—did not develop until considerably later, and so taxes were paid in kind. Tax collection became a major activity of government, requiring a significant bureaucracy to assess and enforce the payment of taxes due. In ancient Mesopotamia, according to a contemporary proverb, the person you should fear the most is the tax collector.

In ancient Greece and Rome, too, a large part of taxation took the form of levies in kind, but taxes of a more recognizably modern form started to appear, in the form of cash levies triggered by certain kinds of transaction, such as the importing of goods, or the sale of land and slaves. During the time of the Roman Republic, extensive use was made of tax farmers, *publicani*, to whom the right to collect taxes for a fixed period of years would be auctioned, giving the Republic a guaranteed steady revenue, while leaving the dirty work of tax collection in the hands of contractors. The writings from this period give plenty of evidence that this was a corrupt and arbitrary system which allowed many *publicani* to enrich themselves greatly, while placing harsh pressures on ordinary taxpayers (Figure 1).

Towards the end of the 1st century BCE, the Roman Emperor Augustus implemented a radical overhaul of the system of taxation, replacing the existing taxes by a fixed property levy, together with a head tax (poll tax) to be levied on the provinces. The censuses that were undertaken to initiate these taxes are familiar from the start of St Luke's Gospel: 'And it came to pass in those days, that

1. Gallo-Roman relief from the 1st century CE showing taxes being paid, from Saintes (France).

there went out a decree from Caesar Augustus, that all the world should be taxed... And all went to be taxed, every one into his own city'. Luke 2:1, 3 (Authorized Version). Likewise, detailed land registers were instituted, recording the ownership of land and its potential productivity. City councils, rather than the *publicani*, now played the primary role in tax collection, and the more predictable and rule-based tax regime catalysed a period of growth and prosperity.

The role of taxation in the subsequent decline and fall of the Roman Empire is heavily disputed. Over many years the fiscal viability of the Roman Empire began to be eroded, caught between the twin blades of rising military costs and a declining yield from taxation, as the provinces that were the main revenue contributors (Figure 1) proved unable—or unwilling—to maintain their massive fiscal transfers to the centre of the Empire. By the

7

3rd century CE, it had become necessary to restrict individual mobility, both geographical and social, to ensure that people did not escape the tax obligations they owed by virtue of their occupation or the land that they farmed. The measures which were taken to extract additional revenues almost certainly hastened the economic decline of the Empire, weakening still further its revenue-raising capacity.

Taxes have waxed and waned over the centuries. In western Europe, the centuries that followed the end of the Roman Empire were marked by a reversion to more rudimentary systems of revenue generation—tithes and the supply of forced labour under the feudal system—that inhibited both economic development and effective government. Taxes of a modern sort—stable and regular levies based on transactions or property—gradually began to reappear, although monarchs frequently resorted to heavy and arbitrary levies when in need of revenue to finance wars or other undertakings. In the early modern period in Europe, social and economic changes began to generate pressures to end arbitrary taxation, and rebellions in a number of European countries started to constrain the power of monarchs to impose taxation at will. Democratic legitimacy in tax policy began to take shape.

Rapid industrialization and democratization in the 19th and 20th centuries have, however, been associated with a dramatic growth in the sophistication of taxation and in the scale of tax revenues in all industrialized countries. At the end of the 19th century tax revenue was less than 10 per cent of national income in both the UK and France, and only about 7 per cent of national income in the United States. During the course of the 20th century, each of these countries then saw substantial growth in the size of the public sector and the burden of taxation, with the share of taxation in overall economic activity increasing roughly by a factor of four. Both world wars appear to have provided significant impetus to the growth of government and the scale of taxation. In the UK, for example, the two world wars were accompanied by a permanent

upward jump in the level of taxation, each time of the order of
10 per cent of national income or so.

Figure 2 shows the growth in the level of overall taxation as a
percentage of gross domestic product (GDP) (i.e. as a share in the

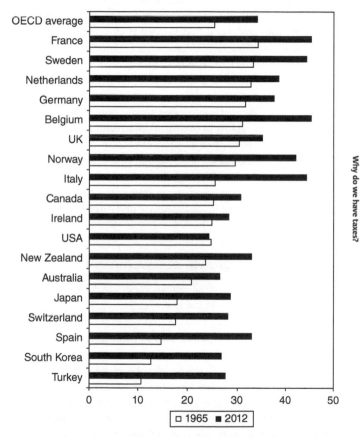

2. **International comparison of the level of taxation, selected countries
(total tax revenues as a percentage of GDP).**

Note: Countries are shown here in descending order of tax as a percentage of
GDP in 1965.

value of overall production) in a number of industrialized countries in 1965 and 2012. Over this period of almost fifty years, different countries have experienced rather different amounts of growth in government spending and taxation. Over the OECD area as a whole, taxation accounted for 25 per cent of GDP in 1965, and 34 per cent in 2012, a growth of nine percentage points. In the UK, growth was only around half this, and the overall burden of taxation in the UK in 2012 was, at 35 per cent of GDP, very close to the OECD average, despite having been substantially higher than the average fifty years earlier. The United States experienced no growth at all in taxation as a percentage of GDP over this period, and by 2012 had the lowest level of taxation, as a percentage of GDP, in any of the countries shown. By contrast, public spending and taxation continued to grow rapidly in some European countries. The level of taxation in France reached 45 per cent of GDP in 2012, a rise of 11 percentage points, and there was an increase of almost twenty points in Italy and Spain. The highest levels of public spending and taxation are almost all in European countries; taxation takes less than 30 per cent of GDP in Japan, Korea, and Australia as well as in the USA.

Taxation and the growth of government

Readers may well differ in their views about the desirability of government spending and taxation on this scale. The proper role of government is, after all, an issue that lies at the heart of political debate and controversy. This short book is not the place to debate this fundamental and complex issue. To a very large extent it should be possible to consider the efficient and equitable design and effective functioning of the tax system, independently of the scale of the revenue-raising task which it is assigned. The features of individual taxes, their economic consequences, the distribution of payments, and their efficient operation are all matters which can be discussed objectively in the light of analysis and evidence of real world operation. In the author's view, much can be learned from the experience of different countries, even where differences in the scale of government demonstrate very different political pressures and underlying philosophies of the role of state action.

However, this is not necessarily a view which is shared by all. Certainly there is a wide measure of agreement across the political spectrum that there are a range of government functions that require tax financing—collective or 'public' goods such as defence and street lighting for which individual charging cannot work. Governments are needed to provide these goods and services, and taxes are required in order to finance them. On the other hand, much of the expansion of government in recent decades has reflected a substantial expansion in the redistributive functions of government. In many countries, especially in Europe, 'welfare state' spending has grown, providing services and income to the poor, the disabled, the sick, and the elderly. Some might argue that the buoyancy of tax revenues at a time of rapid economic growth has made possible growth of government even where there is no pressing need to expand provision of public goods that can be financed only through taxation—that government has become a 'Leviathan', expanding to absorb the resources available.

If this view is taken, it can obviously lead to a very different philosophy of taxation and tax policy. Advocates of efficient revenue-raising might want to reform taxation, to ensure that public revenues can be raised on a fair and efficient basis, with the least disturbance to economic activity and the least possible resistance from taxpayers. To those concerned that efficient taxation invites the excessive growth of government, however, such tax reforms might be seen as unwelcome—as an invitation to government to open its jaw still wider. The latter view—represented, for example, in the economic literature by Brennan and Buchanan amongst others—implies very different priorities in tax policy, with less emphasis on efficiency, and more interest in reforms which would enhance political and constitutional restraints on the taxing powers of government.

Chapter 2
The structure of taxation

Happy families are all alike; each unhappy family is unhappy
in its own way.

Leo Tolstoy, *Anna Karenina*

The tax systems of different countries vary widely. Nearly all share
some common elements, including taxes on personal incomes, sales
taxes, and taxes on corporate profits, each contributing significant
revenues. But beneath these broad similarities lies an extraordinary
diversity in terms of what is taxed by each of the major taxes (the
'tax base'), the rates that are applied, and the legal and practical
aspects of taxation. In addition, while most tax systems rely on
these major taxes for a large proportion of their revenues, most
countries have a diverse range of smaller and not-so-small taxes,
both old and new.

In each country, the present-day tax system reflects a long process
of evolution, in which taxes have been introduced, modified in
response to political pressures, revenue needs, and the experience
of practical operation, and very rarely subject to fundamental review
and coherent modernization. Old taxes tend to survive even when
more modern tax instruments could raise the same revenues more
cheaply and efficiently, simply because tax reform carries political
risks that inhibit change. New taxes may begin life with clear
outlines and a well-defined rationale, but all sorts of idiosyncrasies

and complications can be added over time. As a result, each country's tax system tends to have found its own route to unhappiness—like Tolstoy's unhappy families.

The structure of taxation

To provide an initial benchmark for our discussion of the tax system Figure 3 gives a broad overview of the pattern of taxation in the member countries of the OECD, a grouping which covers thirty-four developed market economies including the USA, Canada, Japan, South Korea, and most member states of the European Union. Figures are shown for 2011, the most recent year for which data is available, and for 1965, the earliest year for which a direct comparison can be made.

About a quarter of total tax revenue in the member states of the OECD is contributed, on average, by the personal income tax, levied on individual incomes from employment and self-employment,

	1965	2011
Personal income tax	26.2	24.1
Social security contributions	17.6	26.2
Other payroll taxes	1.0	1.1
General sales taxes	11.9	20.4
Excises	24.3	10.7
Corporate income tax	8.8	8.7
Property taxes	7.9	5.4
Other taxes	2.3	3.4
Total	**100**	**100**

3. **The structure of taxation in OECD countries, 1965 and 2011** (**percentage shares in total tax revenue**).

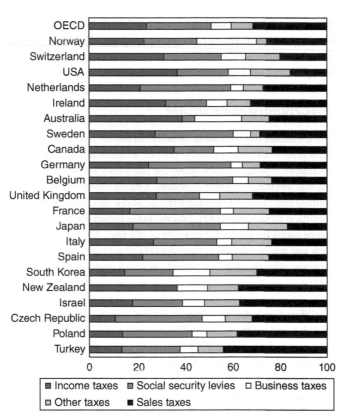

4. The structure of taxation in selected countries, 2011 (percentages of total tax revenues).

Note: Countries are shown here in descending order of per capita GDP, measured at current purchasing power parities (PPPs) (i.e. the 'richest' countries first).

Taxes on income

Income taxes are the most prominent element of the tax system, accounting for about a quarter of all taxes collected in OECD countries.

In view of this prominence, it might be surprising that income taxes were in fact something of a latecomer in the development of modern tax systems (Figure 5). In the United Kingdom, the first income tax was introduced in the late 18th century as a temporary measure to finance the Napoleonic wars, and then quickly abolished. The income tax was reintroduced in 1842, but it was some time before it became fully established as a source of large and broadly stable government revenues.

Income taxes vary widely across countries, both in terms of how the tax base is defined, and in terms of the tax rates applied.

The tax base for the personal income tax in most countries comprises wages and salaries earned by employees, together with other forms of individual income such as rental income from housing and other property, the interest and dividend income that individuals earn from savings and investments, and often income from pensions and state benefits. Most individual income taxes

5. Income taxpayers queuing, New York, 1915. In most industrialized countries the first half of the 20th century saw a significant upward jump in the coverage of the income tax and in the revenue raised.

also apply to the incomes earned by the self-employed, typically allowing the business costs of the self-employed to be deducted before tax is applied to their net trading income.

Beyond this common core, there is much less uniformity. Some countries tax money incomes only; others also apply the income tax to 'income in kind'—such as benefits which an employer may provide to an employee in terms of health care insurance, a company car, luncheon vouchers, free housing, and so forth.

Some countries allow a wide range of deductions against taxable income. Examples include the interest paid on a mortgage and possibly on other forms of loans too, employees' spending on tools and clothing bought for their job, commuting costs, pension contributions, and payments made to purchase health insurance.

Countries differ, too, in how they treat the income of married couples. Some countries operate a regime of joint taxation, in which the incomes of a married couple are combined and taxed together, as a single unit. The UK used to do this—indeed the UK tax system used to treat the income of a married woman as the property of her husband until comparatively recently. In 1990 the UK switched to a system of independent taxation, in which the income tax is applied on an individual basis, and married couples pay the same tax as they would if they were two single individuals.

Once the tax base has been defined, the income tax due can be calculated. It is rare for income tax to be simply proportional to taxpayer income—a single percentage rate applied to all taypayer income. More commonly, different tax rates are applied to successive slices of income—sometimes referred to as tax bands, tax brackets, slabs, or tranches.

In many countries the first slice of income is untaxed. In the United Kingdom, for example, individual taxpayers have a tax-free annual 'allowance' of £10,000, so that if a taxpayer has an income that is less than this they pay no income tax at all. Income tax is then paid—in the UK at a 'basic rate' of 20 per cent—on income above this tax-free allowance. The effect of this is that tax payments rise with taxpayer incomes, beyond the initial allowance, but that the percentage of total income taken in tax is lower than the income tax rate applied. A taxpayer with an income of £11,000 would pay no tax on the first £10,000, and then pay tax at 20 per cent on the remaining £1,000. As a result, their total income tax payment would be £200, only 1.8 per cent of their total income. A taxpayer with an income of £15,000 would pay £1,000 in tax, 6.7 per cent of their total income, and a taxpayer with an income of £30,000 would pay tax of £4,000, 13.3 per cent of their total income.

This illustrates an important distinction, which plays a central role in understanding the distribution of the tax burden and the economic effects of the tax—the distinction between the *average* rate of tax, which is the concept most relevant to questions of fairness or equity in the distribution of the tax burden, and the *marginal* rate of tax, which mainly drives the economic effects.

The average rate of tax is the total tax payment, divided by the total tax base. In the UK case described above this is zero on an income of up to £10,000, and then rises steadily to 13.3 per cent at an income of £30,000.

The marginal rate of tax is the additional tax paid on additional income. It is the *extra* tax that is paid when the taxpayer earns an *extra* pound, dollar, or euro of income. In the UK examples given above, income above the tax-free annual allowance of £10,000 faces a marginal tax rate of 20 per cent.

If the UK's basic rate of 20 per cent applied to all income above the tax-free allowance, then on very high levels of income the average rate of tax would approach 20 per cent. In practice, however, the UK, like most other countries, applies an increasing scale of marginal income tax rates to higher bands of income. So, at an income of around £43,000 a UK taxpayer becomes subject to a higher marginal rate of income tax, 40 per cent, on any additional income, and a still higher marginal rate, of 45 per cent, kicks in when the taxpayer's annual income exceeds £150,000.

A lot of attention is paid in political debate and in the press to the top rates of income tax—in other words to the highest marginal rates. These are usually those charged on the highest band of income, although, as we will see later, poorer households can often face what are in effect very high marginal rates of tax on income.

Income taxes, however, are rarely the only taxes charged on employment incomes. Many countries levy additional income taxes to fund their social insurance systems, in other words, to pay for unemployment and sickness insurance, public pensions, and, in some cases, public health care. In the UK, for example, the system of 'National Insurance Contributions' (NICs) amounts to an additional tax on incomes from employment of more than 20 per cent of income above a tax-free threshold. About half of this is charged to the employee, although—like income tax—collected directly from employers through a system of deduction at source. The remainder is charged to the employer, but, again, based on the payments of wages and salaries to employees. In some countries, social contributions are even larger. In France, for example, social contributions generate revenues which are twice as high as those from the income tax, with the bulk of this being paid by the employer.

As Chapter 3 will show, this distinction between the contributions paid by employer and employee has little, if any, economic substance. Both components amount to a tax on employment incomes, and their economic impact differs little from income tax.

The only sense in which there would be any difference between these contributions and income taxes is if the employee received benefits directly in return, which were proportional to the amounts paid. While many systems may have begun by operating in a way that was in effect an insurance policy, with individual contributions generating an entitlement to a broadly corresponding level of benefit, few countries' social insurance systems look like this nowadays. Most are more properly viewed as a second system of income taxation. In the UK, at least, the portrayal of these charges as 'contributions' has for some time been a misleading fiction, and clearly at odds with the underlying reality.

Taxes on spending

In most countries, taxes on spending include a general, broad-based tax, covering most or all items of consumer spending, and also some additional taxes, or excise duties, on certain individual categories of spending, especially motor fuels, motor vehicles, alcoholic drinks, and tobacco products.

In nearly all OECD countries the general tax on spending takes the form of a VAT. VAT was introduced in France in the 1950s, and adopted by the member countries of the European Community in the late 1960s. It has been one of the great success stories of tax policy in recent years, having now been adopted, in one form or another, by all of the major OECD countries with the exception of the USA, and by many developing countries too.

VAT is levied as a percentage of the value of sales of most goods and services by all forms of business, though in some countries there are exemptions for smaller firms, simply to avoid costs that would be incurred in collecting trivial amounts of tax revenue from a very large number of very small firms. The distinctive feature of VAT is that it generally applies without distinction to sales made to all categories of customers, including sales made to other businesses as well as retail sales to individual consumers. However, businesses which have purchased goods and services from other firms can offset the tax they have paid on these purchases against their VAT bill on their own sales (see Box 1).

Box 1 How VAT works

VAT is charged by firms as a percentage of the value of their sales of goods and services. It applies to all sales, both retail sales to private customers and business-to-business (B2B) trades.

Businesses that buy goods and services bearing VAT can offset the VAT they pay on their purchases against their VAT bill on their own sales. The net effect of this is that only retail sales to consumers end up bearing VAT, since the VAT on B2B trades is, in effect, refunded.

The total VAT revenue collected is equal to the value of retail sales multiplied by the relevant tax rate, but this is collected gradually through the chain of production and distribution.

Example. Consider a simple two-firm chain of production. Firm W weaves cloth, all of which it sells to firm S, who uses the cloth to make suits and sells them to retail customers. Assume the VAT rate is 20%:

	Firm W	*Firm S*
Total sales value	£100,000	£400,000
20% VAT on sales	£20,000	£80,000
Purchased inputs	-	£100,000
VAT paid on inputs	-	£20,000
Net VAT bill	£20,000	£60,000

Total VAT collected = £80,000 (i.e. total revenue = 20% of the value of goods sold to final consumers).

VAT zero-rating means that no tax is charged on sales, but the firm can still claim back VAT paid on inputs.

If the output of firm S in the example is zero-rated, it will charge no VAT on its sales, and receive a net VAT refund of £20,000.

If VAT is a tax on the value of sales, why then is it called a 'value added' tax? The reason can be seen by considering how the tax accumulates during the course of the production chain—as raw materials are gradually transformed into processed materials, components, and then into final products sold to consumers. If the same rate of tax is charged on all sales and purchases, the additional tax collected at each stage of production will be proportional to the value added by that firm: in other words, proportional to the difference between the value of the material and components it buys, and the value of the products it sells.

In practice, most VAT systems have different rates of tax for different categories of goods. Most of the member states of the European Union, for example, have a 'standard' rate of VAT, applying to most goods and services, and one or more 'reduced' rates, applying to particular categories of consumer spending, including food, household energy, books, and newspapers. In France, for example, the standard rate in 2014 was 20 per cent. A reduced rate of 10 per cent applied to public transport, hotels and restaurants, and cultural and sporting events, while food, water, and books were subject to VAT at 5.5 per cent, and newspapers were taxed at 2.1 per cent. The UK too has a standard rate of 20 per cent, but it is unusual in charging a VAT rate of zero on most of the goods subject to reduced rates elsewhere in the EU. Denmark, by contrast, is distinctive in having a single VAT rate. It applies its standard rate of VAT, 25 per cent, across the board to all goods and services.

The USA stands alone among OECD countries in having—so far—resisted the temptations of VAT. Instead, sales are taxed, at state and local level, by a retail sales tax, which applies to sales to retail customers only. Businesses making sales to other businesses as well as to retail customers have to distinguish between the two, and apply the retail sales tax to individual customers, but do not charge the tax on sales to businesses. This 'end user distinction' can be a weakness of a retail sales tax, since the decision may often have to be made by a shopkeeper (or till operator) who may have little reason to ensure that untaxed sales are confined to business customers, and there is little scope for the revenue authorities to monitor the accuracy of these decisions. This vulnerability of retail sales taxes is generally thought to constrain the rates of tax that can be charged, without provoking excessive evasion. Retail sales taxes seem rarely to be charged at rates higher that 10 per cent, while VAT rates of 20 per cent and more are now quite common.

Excise duties were historically one of the main revenue-raising taxes, but have declined in importance over the past century as more modern and powerful broad-based sales taxes have been introduced. Even now, excise duties and taxes on imported goods remain crucial for the revenues of many developing countries, where the organization of economic activity and the limited capacity of government may make complex accounts-based taxes unfeasible.

Excise duties are now confined in most developed countries to a small number of products, including motor fuels, vehicles, alcoholic drinks, and tobacco products. In many countries, some or all of these products are taxed at very high levels indeed. For example, in the UK, the taxes charged on cigarettes, including VAT and the excise duty, account for around 80 per cent of the retail price, while the taxes on petrol amount to nearly 60 per cent of its retail price.

Such high rates of tax require tight control, of the production and distribution of the commodities concerned, if massive tax evasion is not to take place. Generally, excise duties are levied at a relatively early stage in the chain of production and distribution to keep to a minimum the number of businesses involved. It is much easier to charge high levels of tax on whisky by taxing the distiller than it would be to charge similar tax rates at the point of retail sale. Similarly, the high excise duties charged on motor fuels are levied on the major producers, refiners, and importers, and the fuel is only released for distribution and retail sale once the tax has been charged. Nevertheless, while it is relatively straightforward to ensure that large brewers, cigarette manufacturers, and petrol companies are monitored and taxed correctly, the high levels of excise duty can provoke various forms of smuggling, cross-border shopping, and bootleg production. This has become a worrying headache for some revenue authorities in Europe, as border controls have been removed to allow a free flow of trade between the EU member states.

Taxes on business

In many countries, businesses are responsible for a significant part of tax collection—about 90 per cent of revenue in the UK, for example. In nearly all OECD countries employers are required to deduct income taxes and social security contributions 'at source' from the earnings of their employees, even where the legal liability to pay these taxes rests with the employee. In many countries, too, businesses in the financial services sector are required to withhold tax from payments of interest and dividends to investors. In addition to these arrangements for deduction or withholding at source, businesses selling goods and services are usually made responsible for charging any sales taxes which are due on the transaction, and for remitting the sales tax revenues to the tax authorities.

These major taxes are taxes on business only in a pragmatic sense, in that businesses are simply being used as convenient—and unpaid—tax collectors. In addition, however, two groups of taxes are levied on business in a more substantial sense, in that the amounts that the business pays in tax are related in a more fundamental way to the characteristics of the business and its organization.

First, there are taxes on corporate profits, such as the UK's corporation tax. These are levied on incorporated businesses—those that have a legal status independent of the individual shareholders who own the business. There is enormous variation between countries in how the profit of a business is defined for tax purposes, especially how the costs of finance and investment are treated. These differences in the definition of the base for corporate profits taxes may have very large effects on the amount of taxes due, which may be at least as significant as the rate of tax in determining the overall corporate tax burden in different countries. Nevertheless, a lot of attention is paid to the rate of corporation tax, and many countries have cut the tax rate, hoping that this might attract investment from internationally footloose businesses.

Corporate profits taxes have been at the centre of great controversy in recent years, focusing on the accounting devices used by some major corporations—Amazon, Apple, and Starbucks amongst others—to minimize the taxes they pay in some major markets and to shift taxable profits to lower tax or tax-haven countries. We return to this issue later.

In addition to taxes on corporate profits, many countries also levy other taxes on business activity, property, or assets. The UK levies a substantial tax on the value of business property and fixed assets called *business rates*. Originally a tax levied by local government, this tax in effect became part of the national tax system when, in 1990, the government decided that local authorities should lose the power to set the rate of tax to be paid by businesses in their area. The tax is substantial—raising more than 4 per cent of total UK tax revenues—and the amount of tax payable is unaffected by the level of profits earned by the business. In effect, business rates impact on businesses in very much the same way as property rents: they are a fixed cost of occupying premises, which has to be covered before any profits are earned. Although the particular idiosyncrasies of the UK's system of business rates are not encountered in other tax systems, many countries levy some form of tax on business assets or business activity, often taking the form of a municipal tax, locally set and contributing revenues to finance the local government budget.

Other taxes

This category includes taxes and levies on the ownership or transfer of financial assets and physical property, taxes on wealth and inheritance, taxes on the use of natural resources and on environmental damage, taxes on international trade (Figure 6), and a kaleidoscopic array of miscellaneous fees, licences, and permits.

Taxes on physical property are often among the oldest parts of a country's tax system. Land and buildings are easy to define,

6. 'Duty Paid' by Ralph Hedley (1848–1913). Import duties were a significant revenue source for many countries in the 19th century, but play little role in revenue-raising today, except in some developing countries.

virtually impossible to hide, and their ownership is often a matter of public record. It is quite common for property taxes to be levied by local government, as property can be uniquely allocated to a particular location, while it would be much harder to assign most other taxes so clearly to a particular jurisdiction. Property taxes could be levied simply on the basis of measures of physical size—such as an amount per square metre of floor-space or acre of land—but most property taxes have evolved to reflect the value of the property and not just its size. The UK's Council Tax, a tax on domestic property which is levied by local governments, is based on an assessment of the market value of each property, undertaken when the tax was introduced in 1993.

Many countries raise significant amounts of money by taxing transactions in physical assets such as land and buildings. The UK, for example, levies a Stamp Duty when houses are sold, and similar taxes on housing transactions are found in many other countries. Stamp duties and other taxes on sale can also be levied on transactions in various financial assets, such as stocks and shares.

In addition to taxes on physical property and on asset transactions, a few countries levy taxes on wealth—in other words on the value of physical and financial assets that an individual or household owns. France, for example, levies an annual wealth tax on households with net assets in excess of €1.3 million, at rates of 0.5 per cent to 1.5 per cent of the asset value. About a quarter of a million households are subject to this tax, which contributes less than 2 per cent of overall tax receipts.

Taxes on inheritance have a long history, again because the state is often involved in regulating or certifying the will of a deceased person, and the arrangements for the disposal of their estate. If some legal process is required to certify the assets owned by someone who has died, or the arrangements for their distribution, it is a relatively small step to charging a levy on the certified value of the assets left by the deceased.

Countries that have large deposits of oil and mineral resources can collect substantial revenues in the form of resource taxes, extraction licences, or royalty fees. Many of the major oil-producing countries are able to afford lavish public spending while maintaining tax rates on individual income and spending at very low rates. Indeed none of the Gulf states, Qatar, United Arab Emirates, Bahrain, and Kuwait, has an income tax at all, although local residents all pay—relatively modest—social security taxes. Since the 1970s, the development of the oil and gas reserves in the North Sea has generated significant revenues for the UK, although these have declined in recent years as the most profitable fields have been exhausted, and the UK government has reduced taxation to try to encourage oil companies to invest in the costly development of more inaccessible fields. Norway and the Netherlands, too, have both benefited from tax revenues from oil and gas fields. For Norway, these revenues continue to be very large in relation to the public budget, and—rather than blowing the money on a short-term binge of lavish spending and low taxation—successive Norwegian governments have prudently invested this revenue windfall in a massive sovereign wealth fund, to ensure that the country benefits from a continuing flow of income once the oil runs out.

A growing awareness of environmental issues has led many countries to introduce tax measures to discourage pollution and environmental damage. Existing taxes, such as those on carbon-based fuels and motor vehicles, have been increased or restructured to discourage the most polluting activities or stimulate the take-up of greener alternatives. In addition, new taxes have been introduced specifically to address particular environmental problems—for example the UK's Landfill Tax on waste dumps, introduced in 1996 with the aim of encouraging greater recycling.

Finally, there is one area of taxation which has declined sharply over the last half-century, especially in the industrialized world. Tariffs on international trade—taxes on imported goods—have been reduced to very low levels as a result of the successive rounds of multilateral tariff reductions agreed under the auspices of the World Trade Organization (WTO), and its predecessor, the General Agreement on Tariffs and Trade (GATT). In the United States and in the EU the revenue from tariffs is now only about 1 per cent of the revenue from other taxes. Elsewhere, however, and especially in less developed countries, the significance of tariff revenues can be much greater. For countries with limited administrative capacity, frontier formalities provide one of the few reliable points at which taxes can be charged, and import taxes can make a significant and secure contribution to public revenues. In many countries in Africa, tariffs contribute 20 per cent or more of total tax revenues.

Chapter 3
Who bears the tax burden?

How much tax do you pay? Perhaps your employer deducts income tax from your wages, and you pay little attention to your payslip apart from the bottom line—the net amount that goes into your bank account. Alternatively you may be required to calculate and pay your own income tax each year, and may be only too familiar with the size of your income tax bill. But we have seen that income tax accounts for only about a quarter of the total tax revenue collected in OECD countries. What about all the other taxes that are levied? How much of them ends up coming out of your pockets?

And how does the amount of tax you pay compare with what others pay—those better off than you and those who are poorer? 'Who pays the tax?' is an endlessly fascinating question—and an issue on which people can feel very strongly.

'Formal' and 'effective' incidence

It might be thought that if we levy a tax on a particular group of individuals they would be the people who would bear the burden of the tax. So, if we tax farmers, then it is farmers who are made poorer by the tax; if we levy a tax on shopkeepers, then it is the living standard of shopkeepers that falls, and so on. One of the crucial insights that economic analysis provides to tax policy is that this is far from the truth. The real burden of a tax can be borne somewhere completely different from the location of the legal liability to pay the tax.

The economic perspective on taxation distinguishes between the 'formal' and 'effective' (or 'economic') incidence of a tax. Formal incidence is a matter of who is legally liable to pay the tax, or from whom the tax is collected. Effective incidence concerns the more fundamental question of who ultimately bears the burden of the tax. One way of thinking about effective incidence is to ask, 'Whose living standard falls as a result of the tax?' This may not always be the same person on whom the tax is formally incident. The imposition of a tax can affect demand or supply in the markets for goods, labour, or capital, and hence it can change prices, wages, or interest rates. These economic adjustments can have the effect of shifting the burden of a tax away from its formal incidence, so that some or all of the burden is transferred away from the firm or individual who is legally liable to pay it.

Moreover, the outcome will be the same, regardless of whether the tax is imposed on the buyer or the seller. In a competitive market, formal incidence does not merely differ from the final economic incidence, it is *irrelevant* in determining economic incidence. It doesn't matter whether we tax the buyer or the seller: the quantity traded, the tax-inclusive price paid by the buyer, and the net-of-tax payment received by the seller will all be the same.

Many countries impose a tax, such as the UK's Stamp Duty, on the sale of private houses. In some countries the buyer is legally responsible for paying this tax—in others, it is the seller. This assignment of legal liability ensures that there is no confusion over who should make the payment, but it should have no effect on the housing market or on the individual transactions that take place. We would expect the price at which any sale is made to take full account of who has to pay the tax, so that the selling price would be higher, by the exact amount of the tax, if the seller is responsible for paying the tax rather than if the liability falls on the buyer. What determines whether a potential buyer is willing to sign the proposed contract of sale is the total amount that has to be paid, and the buyer is unlikely to care whether this accrues to the seller or to the government; likewise what governs whether the seller is willing to agree to sell their house is the net amount they will receive from the sale. Neither of these two crucial values is affected by the assignment of legal liability to pay the tax on the sale.

The observation that the economic outcome of a tax is unaffected by its legal incidence has some immediate, and rather convenient, implications for policy. It allows us, for example, to choose the side of the market on which to levy a sales tax simply on the basis of administrative cost and convenience. Sales taxes are much more conveniently imposed on the sellers of goods, since there are fewer of them than customers, and it is easier to require them to keep detailed records of transactions which can then be used as the basis for levying sales taxes. Fortunately, exploiting this convenience in administration does not at the same time require us to accept that sellers should be burdened with more of the incidence of the tax; that is governed by economic substance, and is unaffected by our administrative choices.

Part or all of the burden of a sales tax will be borne by customers, if businesses increase their prices to cover the tax payment. How much of the sales tax is passed on to consumers will depend on features of the particular market. In a competitive market, the extent to which a retail sales tax is shifted forwards to customers will depend on how much the supply of the commodity (by producers) and the demand for the commodity (by consumers) respond to changes in its price. Putting this in economic jargon, it will be governed by the relative 'elasticities' of supply and demand for the taxed commodity. If taxes are imposed on the sale of products where consumer spending is very responsive to the product price, relatively little of the tax will be incident on

33

consumers, and correspondingly more of the burden of the tax will be borne by producers. By contrast, the burden of a tax imposed on a product whose supply is very responsive to price, while consumer demand is insensitive to price, will tend to fall more on the purchasers of the product than on its producers.

Readers who have previously encountered the notions of economic supply and demand curves may find that the economic processes underpinning these economic adjustments can be grasped more readily in the context of a simple diagram. For these readers—and for others who are intrigued by the concepts and apparatus of economic analysis—a supply-and-demand curve diagram is provided in Figure 7 and discussed in Box 2. For those readers who have not been initiated into the formal arts of economics, the crucial insight reflected in this diagram is that the prices at which goods and services are bought and sold in a market economy reflect an interaction between, on the one hand, the opportunities for profitable supply, and, on the other, the

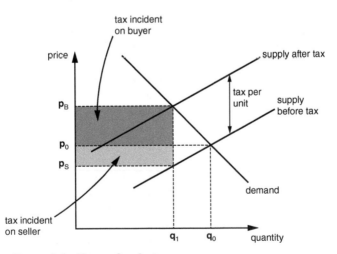

7. **Economic incidence of a sales tax.**

Box 2 The economic incidence of a sales tax: interpretation of Figure 7

Figure 7 shows the supply and demand curves for a good in a competitive market, before and after the imposition of a sales tax per unit sold. In the absence of taxation, the market is in equilibrium at a price p_o and quantity q_o. The imposition of a tax on each unit sold shifts the supply curve upwards by the full amount of the tax per unit. Following the imposition of the tax the price that balances supply and demand will be p_B, and the quantity sold will fall to q_1.

At this lower quantity, the price that the seller receives is p_S, while the price the buyer pays is p_B. The difference between the two prices is the amount of the tax per unit. The total tax collected is the area of the full shaded rectangle (the tax, multiplied by the quantity sold). Part of this is borne by the buyer, who now pays a higher price for each unit purchased. The incidence of the tax on the buyer is represented by the darker shaded area. The remainder of the tax is borne by the seller, who now receives a lower price per unit, after tax. The incidence of the tax on the seller is shown by the lighter shaded area.

The division of the incidence of the tax between buyer and seller depends on the relative slopes of the demand and supply curves. If the demand curve is steeper than the supply curve (i.e. demand is less price-sensitive than supply), more of the incidence will be borne by the buyer, as in the example here.

strength of consumer demand at different price levels. Where the market price ends up—the 'equilibrium' price, in the jargon—is determined by the balance between these two pressures, and this outcome will be influenced by the imposition of the tax.

The extent to which a sales tax collected from sellers is shifted forwards to consumers in higher prices is the outcome of a market process in which supply and demand in the market is rebalanced. The final outcome may be reached quickly, or it may take some time to be achieved, especially if it is costly for firms to adjust prices, or if buyers and sellers are locked into existing contracts for a period of time. Tax shifting is not necessarily the outcome of conscious or deliberate decisions by sellers or other market participants, nor is it a process that can, to any real extent, be regulated by law. Certainly some governments do on occasion try to control the way in which changes in taxes feed through into the prices paid by consumers, but this is a largely quixotic enterprise, liable to be frustrated by the price adjustments that sellers will naturally make in response to changing costs and consumer demands.

In a competitive market, then, the effective incidence of a tax on sales is governed by the relative responsiveness of supply and demand to changes in price. Once we move away from fully competitive markets, however, the economic processes that determine tax incidence become much more complicated. Where the burden of a sales tax lies will depend on the market structure, the pricing behaviour of firms within the market, and on other details of demand, supply, and the precise specification of the tax. In the case of a product sold by a single monopoly supplier, for example, relatively small changes in the characteristics of supply can result in the tax being shifted more or less than in a competitive market. Cases of shifting in excess of 100 per cent are possible, where a tax would induce the monopolist to increase prices by more than the tax, shifting all of the tax and more to consumers. In markets where there are a small number of firms with a degree of market power falling short of complete monopoly, the strategic interactions between firms' pricing decisions can become extremely complex and varied. In some such markets, a firm that raises its price may find that other firms leave their prices unchanged in order to grab as much market share as possible. In this case, a sales tax would be likely to be fully incident on the firms. Alternatively, however, firms in such an imperfectly competitive market might follow each others' lead, all raising their own prices to match any price increase made by a competitor. In this case, the full burden of any sales tax would fall on consumers.

The logic of this analysis applies equally well to the labour market. A tax on wages will have an effect on the cost of labour to employers and on the living standards of workers that will be governed by the relative elasticities of labour supply and demand. The available evidence on the labour supply of men in the workforce suggests that their hours of work vary very little in response to changes in wages. This would suggest that, at least in areas of employment dominated by men, the bulk of the incidence of taxes on labour income will be borne by the workers, and not by their employer. As we will discuss in the next chapter there is rather more evidence that the working hours of women, especially those with young children, respond much more to changes in the wage rate. In areas of the labour market where women form a significant part of the labour force, this greater responsiveness of hours of work to wage rates will tend to reduce the proportion of a tax on wages that will be borne by employees.

The irrelevance of formal incidence to economic incidence also applies to taxes on the labour market. Again this means we can levy taxes on whichever side of the market is most convenient, without any implications for where the final burden of wage taxes will lie. It also has a dramatic implication for one of the major revenue-raising taxes in most countries' tax systems: the payroll taxes levied to finance social security systems. Many countries divide these into a portion 'paid' by the employer and a proportion 'paid' by the employee, although frequently these two elements are both collected from employers in exactly the same way. From an economic point of view this distinction is an absurdity, and the time that is spent debating the appropriate balance between employer and employee contributions to social insurance is time wasted in a discussion of no real economic substance. The only sense in which the economic effects of the two components might be likely to differ is in the very short term, following a change in the tax rates, before the labour market has fully adjusted to the change in taxes. Economic decisions of employers, however, reflect the tax-inclusive labour cost, including the effect of both contributions, and the labour market decisions of employees reflect the after-tax wage, after all contributions and taxes. No decision of economic substance hinges on the balance between the two elements.

The incidence of taxes on real estate—taxes on land and buildings—can also be understood in a similar way. Land, in general, is in fixed supply, and any taxes on sales of land, therefore, are incident on the seller rather than the buyer. Likewise, we would expect any taxes on land rents to be incident on the landowner, and not on the tenant. Legislation cannot alter this; in a competitive market it is a natural and unavoidable outcome.

With buildings, incidence will be more complex. The supply is almost fixed in the short-term, as new construction in any year is unlikely to add more than a small percentage to the total stock of housing or of office-space. Over a longer run horizon, however, significant new construction can take place, and this additional supply will shift more of the burden of taxes on the ownership or occupation of residential or commercial property towards the occupiers rather than the owners.

A further feature of taxes on land—and, for that matter, assets in general—should be noted. Taxes in current and future years are all likely to be reflected in the current price of the asset, since any sale of the asset effectively also hands over to the new owner the liability to pay all future taxes. Even if the owner only expects to hold the asset for a year or two, they will anticipate that, when they come to sell the asset, the purchaser, too, will think of the costs of ownership in these terms. The future taxes will reduce correspondingly the amount they are willing to pay. So, the effect is to make all future taxes incident on the current owner—a phenomenon known as capitalization. A tax reform that imposes a new tax on an asset will be immediately reflected in a fall in the asset's value, equal to the net present value of the tax in current and all future years. New taxes on assets therefore impose heavy burdens on current owners. Likewise, abolishing asset taxes confers windfall gains on whoever currently happens to own them without in any way reducing the costs of the asset to any future owner (who will now have to pay a higher price to buy the asset, which will wipe out any benefit from the reduced future tax liability). Governments tempted to change the tax treatment of assets should bear these effects in mind. Tax reforms can impose capricious and unjustified windfall gains or losses on the current owners of long-lived assets, and substantial harm can be done by tax policy-making that fails to recognize these effects.

And what of corporate profits taxes? Where does their incidence lie? On shareholders? On customers? On employees? Only one thing is clear: the burden of taxes on business does not end up 'on business'. Ultimately all taxes on business are borne somewhere else, and ultimately by individuals.

Tracing the ultimate burden of taxes on business assets and profits is much more complex than in the case of taxes on sales and incomes, and the findings of research do not reach the same level of consensus about where the effective incidence of tax in practice lies. The issues involved go well beyond the simple analytical framework which we have used to discuss the effects of other taxes—the so-called 'partial equilibrium' framework, in which we discuss the effects of the tax simply in terms of the market to which it is applied. For taxes on corporate profits we need to look at a wider set of economic interactions, including individual savings and investment decisions, the supply of capital to both incorporated and unincorporated businesses, and the possible interactions with both the labour market and product markets.

On one view, taxes on corporate profits simply amount to additional taxation of the income that will eventually accrue to shareholders. Indeed, this view was, at one time, reflected quite explicitly in the tax systems of a number of countries, by crediting the corporate tax that the company had paid to the company's individual shareholders, allowing them to reduce correspondingly their individual income tax liability.

More recently, however, research has begun to assemble a growing body of evidence showing that a significant part of the burden of taxes on corporate profits ends up being borne by employees. The processes underlying this are complex, but at least two mechanisms seem to be involved. One is an observation that bargaining over wages between workers and their employers can often succeed in securing for the workers a share of the benefits of particular competitive advantages that their firm might possess; to the extent that these benefits are reduced by taxation of the firm's profits, the workers may be able to secure less. The second mechanism has particularly dramatic implications for tax policy. It operates in 'small' economies that are exposed to international competition for capital—probably most of the economies in the world these days. A 'small' economy in this discussion is not a country with limited area or population, but a country whose use of capital does not have any appreciable impact on the global cost of capital. Instead, the country's firms have to compete for capital with locations abroad, and any taxation of the return to capital will simply reduce the amount of capital that they can attract. The effect is to shift the burden of taxation of capital in such a country away from capital (which would otherwise simply move elsewhere) to domestic tax bases which are less mobile—probably, therefore, to wages.

Distributional incidence

So, we have seen, in broad terms, where the burden of the major taxes will lie. Income taxes and payroll taxes are likely to be borne largely by employees, a major part of the burden of taxes on sales is likely to be passed on to customers, and, while the burden of corporate profits taxes is complex and unclear, there are good reasons for believing that in a relatively small open economy a significant part of the corporate profit tax burden actually ends up being borne by employees, through reduced real wages, rather than by internationally mobile capital.

But how large is the tax burden borne on average by each taxpayer? And how is it distributed across different groups of individuals or households? In particular, how is the tax burden distributed between households with different levels of income—in other words, how is the burden distributed between rich and poor?

Research on these questions has expanded dramatically in recent decades, as techniques have been developed for simulating the impact of taxes using large-scale survey datasets covering thousands of households. This has made it possible to build up a much more detailed picture of the impact of taxation on household living standards, and how different taxes are distributed across the population. These questions are fascinating from a purely intellectual point of view. But for the tax policy-maker, there are two particular reasons to want to understand how the tax burden is distributed across households.

The first is that, in making judgements about tax policy, policy-makers may have considerations of equity or fairness in mind. Many tax policy choices, as we will see at various places in this book, involve a trade-off between the efficiency of revenue-raising, and the equity of the outcome, in terms of the distribution of the burden of taxation between rich and poor. Sometimes the taxes that one might wish to choose, purely from the standpoint of economic and operational efficiency, are taxes that bear particularly heavily on poorer households. Policy-makers then need to judge how far, with any particular tax, it is worth sacrificing some efficiency for the sake of greater equity in the overall burden of tax payments.

A second reason that policy-makers and politicians are so interested in the impact of taxes on different groups of households is much more pragmatic. It would be wise to know who will be the losers from any tax reform, and how badly they will be affected, before embarking on policy proposals and legislation. Otherwise legislators could find themselves badly bruised when voters who have been the losers from tax reform subsequently take their electoral revenge.

Economics has developed some terminology to characterize the impact of taxes at different levels of income, which is widely used—and quite often mis-used—in policy debate. It takes as its baseline a tax that is exactly proportional to income—in other words, a situation where the amount taken from each household in tax is the same proportion of income at all income levels. Selecting this as a baseline does not mean there is something particularly appropriate, desirable, or sacred about exact proportionality of tax payments to household income; it is simply a convenient starting point for analysing a range of patterns of tax payment in relation to income.

Then, two different distributional patterns of tax payments are given particular names. A 'progressive' tax is one where a household's tax payments increase as a percentage of income as incomes rise, while a regressive tax has the opposite relationship between tax payments and income: the share of income taken in tax is higher at low levels of income. It is perhaps unfortunate that, back in the mists of time, words were chosen to characterize the distribution of income that carry particularly favourable and pejorative overtones, respectively, and that would also have a useful meaning quite separate from the discussion of the impact of taxes on households at different standards of living. Sometimes this can lead to confusion, especially when advocates of some particular reform wish to argue that what they propose is 'progressive', irrespective of the evidence about its impact on the tax burden. In this book, the terms are employed as a convenient way of summarizing the relationship between tax burden and income.

Different readers will no doubt have their own views about the extent to which public policies should seek to redistribute income between rich and poor. This is a matter of moral judgement, a question of 'fairness' about which rational, well-informed people may disagree, even while agreeing about facts such as the current distribution of the tax burden and the pattern of payments of different taxes. The priority that *should* be given to distributional equity in the design of public policies, including taxation, goes to the heart of different philosophies about politics and society. I have my own views about this, and I am sure that to some extent they are evident to the reader from the policy issues that I have chosen to discuss in this book. Readers may well disagree, and are entitled to their own moral views—value judgements—about what should be done. Such judgements are a matter of individual principle and preference, and the desirability of redistribution cannot be 'proved' by the description of facts—still less, by the choice of vocabulary.

In the tax systems of most advanced countries, income taxes tend to have a significantly progressive distributional pattern. It is rare for income taxes to be set exactly proportional to income, at all points on the income scale. Most income tax systems try to mitigate the burden of tax on poorer households in various ways. One way of doing this, reflected in the tax systems of many countries, is to levy higher percentage 'marginal' rates of tax on successive slices of a taxpayer's income. Another is to exempt an initial slice of taxpayer income from tax altogether—as in the UK income tax system described in the previous chapter. Both have the effect that a household's tax payments rise more rapidly than income, so that the share of income taken in tax increases at higher income levels.

By contrast, the distributional pattern of sales tax payments tends to be much less progressive, and in many countries can be quite sharply regressive. The pattern of sales tax burden across households will depend on the pattern of household spending, and the tax rates applied to different goods and services. Unlike direct taxes, where tax rates can be related directly to household income, the burden of indirect taxes is related to household income only to the extent that the spending patterns of poor and rich households differ. Some of the regressivity arises because households in the poorest income groups spend more and save less of their income, and some arises when poorer households' spending contains a higher proportion of heavily taxed items. We return to this issue shortly.

Some recent estimates from the Institute for Fiscal Studies (IFS) of the distribution of the household tax burden in the UK are summarized in Figure 8. This chart, based on a large-scale official survey of household income and spending patterns and detailed estimates of household tax payments calculated by the IFS tax and benefit simulation model, allocates to households most of the major UK taxes, including income tax, National Insurance contributions (including those formally incident on the employer, for the reasons discussed earlier in this chapter), the council tax, levied to finance local government, and taxes on spending, including VAT and excises. Due to uncertainties about incidence, business taxes including corporation tax and business rates are excluded, as are capital taxes, including inheritance tax and capital gains tax. Overall the analysis covers about three-quarters of all UK tax revenue.

In the chart, households are lined up in increasing order of disposable income, and then divided into ten equal sized groups—the 'decile groups'—each comprising 10 per cent of all UK households. The poorest 10 per cent of households are shown on the far left of the graph, and subsequent decile groups are in increasing order of household income, with the richest 10 per cent of the population on the far right. The chart shows the average tax payments of households in each income group, and the

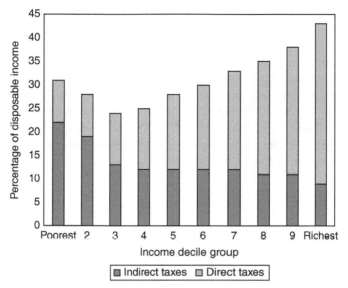

8. Who pays the taxes? Distribution of direct and indirect taxes by decile groups of household income, United Kingdom, 2009–10.

Note: Taxes on spending include VAT and excise taxes. Taxes on income include income tax, employee and employer National Insurance contributions, and council tax. Excludes corporation tax, business rates, and capital taxes.

breakdown between two different groups of taxes, 'indirect taxes' levied on the sale of goods and services, which burden households indirectly through their purchases, and 'direct taxes', which are principally those levied on income.

At the very bottom end of the income distribution, the pattern of tax payments is regressive. For the poorest 10 per cent of the population, taxes are 31 per cent of income, falling to 28 per cent in the second decile, and 24 per cent in the third. Thereafter, across the rest of the income range the tax burden is progressive, and the percentage of income taken in tax rises steadily with higher household income, to reach about 43 per cent of income for the richest 10 per cent of households.

A contrast can be seen between the distribution of payments of the direct and indirect taxes. The indirect taxes, VAT and excises, together have a sharply regressive distributional effect, with tax payments of 22 per cent of income for the poorest 10 per cent of households, falling steadily across the income range, to less than half this percentage—only 9 per cent—among the richest 10 per cent. By contrast, the direct taxes levied on income increase steadily as a proportion of income throughout the income distribution, from 9 per cent of income in the bottom decile to 34 per cent of income in the top decile.

Two key points should be highlighted. First, the figure illustrates the importance of looking at the tax system as a whole in considering the distributional impact of different taxes. If what we are interested in is the impact of the tax system on the standard of living that can be maintained by households at lower levels of income, the right focus of our attention is the overall impact of the tax system, and not the distributional impact of individual taxes. It is possible for the regressive effect of one tax within the overall tax system to be offset by the effect of other taxes with a more progressive distribution. Except for the bottom two deciles this is broadly true of the tax burden as a whole in the UK: the regressive impact of the indirect taxes is more than offset by the more strongly progressive impact of the direct taxes.

Second, the figure concentrates on taxes alone. However, it is very difficult to understand the impact of taxes in the UK system—and in many other countries' tax systems—without taking into account how they interact with systems of social protection for poor households, the unemployed, disabled, and pensioners. In the UK system, many of these state 'benefits' are income-related, or based on a 'means test'—an assessment of individual or household income, so that they are only paid to households with low incomes and not to all households. Some of the payments directly relate to tax payments—for example, housing benefits cover part of the council tax that a poor household would otherwise pay—and low-income households receive benefits that significantly offset the effect of income tax. More generally, redistribution through the pattern of taxation and through social benefits provides alternative routes to providing support for poorer households, and it is difficult to argue that we should pay attention to only one part of this, the tax burden, while disregarding the role of benefits. For this reason, the Mirrlees Review, from which these data were drawn, shows the overall impact of taxes and benefits taken together—a pattern which is strongly progressive throughout the income scale, offsetting, on average at least, the regressivity of the tax burden on poorer households.

Chapter 4
Taxation and the economy

It is the part of the good shepherd to shear his flock, not flay it.

Tiberius Caesar

Taxation in the provinces of the Roman empire was notorious for its severity. Heavy taxes were levied on the provinces to finance the central administration of the empire and its huge military machine, and during costly military campaigns the tax burden could be increased dramatically. At times taxation reached levels that made agriculture and trade unprofitable, and laws were needed to prevent farmers simply leaving the land to escape the burden of taxation. The harm done by arbitrary and excessive taxation was apparent to many observers, and, as Suetonius records, even to the emperor Tiberius Caesar.

Modern tax systems involve much greater clarity and transparency than the arbitrary systems of revenue generation in the Roman provinces. However, the level of taxation in most developed countries is sufficiently high that badly designed tax policies can cause significant economic harm. Many OECD countries have high standards of social protection against the risks of unemployment and sickness, and make costly public provision for the costs of old age. These public policy choices require high levels of taxation on incomes and spending. In OECD countries taxes take on average 34 per cent of the value of national output, and in countries with particularly high standards of social protection such as Sweden and France the tax burden exceeds 40 per cent of GDP. In this chapter we look at the economic costs of taxation, and show how these are not simply a matter of the amount of tax that is paid.

The economic costs of taxation

Taxation transfers resources—money—from taxpayers to the government. In the process, economic costs of three main sorts are incurred.

First, there are resources that have to be spent by government in operating the tax system—the 'administrative costs' of taxation. In most countries the budget of the tax agency constitutes the largest part of these costs, although costs may also be incurred in tax collection by other levels of government. The operating costs of the Internal Revenue Service (IRS) in the United States are, for example, about $40 per head of population; in the United Kingdom, the annual budget for Her Majesty's Revenue and Customs (HMRC) is the equivalent of approximately £75 per head. In both countries, these operating costs amount to less than 1 per cent of the total tax revenue collected.

Second, taxpayers incur costs in their interactions with the tax system, including the time spent filling in tax returns and in correspondence with the revenue authorities, and, in some cases, the costs of employing a tax accountant. For complex taxes, in particular, these 'compliance costs' incurred by taxpayers can be substantial.

Evidence on the scale and pattern of taxpayer compliance costs is quite patchy. In the United States it has been estimated that individual taxpayers spend on average about twenty-seven hours each year in dealing with state and local income taxes; self-employed taxpayers, whose affairs tend to be more complex, spend on average sixty hours a year. This time has a cost in the sense that it could instead have been spent working, or on more pleasurable activities. Valuing the cost of taxpayer time, and adding the cost of accountants, gives a total tax compliance cost of some $80 billion for the US personal income tax alone, equivalent to about $250 per head of population.

The UK income tax system, by contrast, requires relatively few taxpayers to fill in an annual tax return—most are taxed entirely through the Pay-As-You-Earn (PAYE) system operated by their employers. This means that a substantial proportion of tax compliance costs are borne by employers. Estimating tax compliance costs incurred by employers is particularly difficult, because it is difficult to disentangle the time spent on tax activities from financial accounting that would be needed even in the absence of taxes. However, it seems likely that overall compliance costs for the UK personal income tax and social contributions amount to at least £3.4 billion annually, about £60 per head of population, or 1.3 per cent of the revenue collected. The compliance costs of the other major UK taxes, corporation tax and VAT, are significantly higher in relation to revenues, at 2 per cent and nearly 4 per cent, respectively.

Third, there are more subtle costs of taxation, which arise because taxation can alter the way in which people and firms behave. These changes in individual decisions and behaviour are costly in the sense that people are induced by the presence of taxes to do things that they would not choose to do in the absence of taxation. Economists refer to these effects as the distortionary effects of taxes, and the economic value of these tax-induced changes in individual decisions as the distortionary costs of taxation.

Taken together, the costs of tax distortions in individual behaviour can be summarized in the notion of the excess burden of taxation. This reflects the idea that taxes which affect behaviour impose costs on taxpayers—and hence on the economy—over and above the money which is collected in tax. 'Excess burden' is a way of measuring this economic harm from distortionary taxation, and a well-designed tax system would aim to raise required revenues while keeping excess burden to a minimum. Economists refer to this as 'efficiency' in revenue-raising: raising a given revenue at the lowest possible distortionary cost.

In thinking about public policy, we might be particularly interested in the marginal excess burden of raising additional revenues through taxation—in other words, the extra distortionary cost incurred in raising each additional pound in tax revenue. Estimates of excess burden vary widely, but as a rough rule of thumb, taxes in most industrialized countries might have a marginal excess burden of at least 30 pence for each £1 raised in tax, and badly designed taxes considerably more than this.

Efficiency and 'excess burden'

In some cases the distortionary costs of taxation are clear and obvious. When, in 1696, a 'window tax' was introduced in England, charging people by the number of windows in the property they occupied, it was no doubt seen as a tax that would be easy to assess, and that would distribute the burden of taxation roughly in proportion to the wealth of different taxpayers. However, one of the side-effects of the tax was to induce householders to brick up some of their windows, so as to reduce the tax that they would have to pay. Some of these blocked-up windows can be seen to this day, visible reminders of the way in which taxes can affect individual behaviour. The costs of this tax-induced blocking up of windows are in principle obvious: people sacrificed a certain amount of light and comfort in order to save tax, living in darker and less attractive accommodation than they would have chosen if the tax had not been levied (Figure 9). To measure the cost of this disamenity we would need to understand more about the amount of discomfort and unhappiness that people suffered, living in homes with blocked-up windows, but we can at least put an upper limit on the value of the disamenity. The people who blocked up their windows presumably valued the tax saving more highly than the forgone light and comfort from the windows they lost.

51

A VISION OF THE REPEAL OF THE WINDOW-TAX.
"Hollo! Old Fellow; we're glad to see you here."

9. **The distortionary costs of taxation. In this 1850 cartoon from *Punch* a working-class father and his family look forward to the repeal of the Window Tax, which had led many householders and landlords to block up windows to save tax.**

Similarly, when we see people doing things 'just for tax reasons', it is an indication that the tax system involves distortion and waste. For example, when we see people spending time and money in pursuit of a tax saving—for example, when people make costly trips across the English Channel to buy wine and beer in France because it is taxed less—these are resources which are being wasted as a result of taxation.

However, these very obvious cases of tax-induced distortions in individual behaviour are only the tip of a very much larger iceberg. Most taxes which are levied have the potential to modify and influence individual behaviour. Taxes on goods and services affect product prices and influence what people buy. Taxes on labour income influence how much people work. Taxes on income from savings can influence how much people save, or the form in which they choose to save. Taxes on company profits can influence a whole range of corporate decisions: where the company is based, how it is owned and financed, how much it invests, how much it produces, and how many people it employs. All of these effects of taxes on individual and firm behaviour imply that costs are being incurred in the course of raising revenue through taxation. People and firms are doing things differently to what they would choose in the absence of taxation. These changes in behaviour are a cost of taxation, in just the same way that the bricked-up windows caused costs to householders in the form of discomfort and disamenity.

The most straightforward context in which to see the economic impact of tax distortion is when a tax is levied on the sale of one particular product. (For those who wish to see the following analysis in diagrammatic terms, with supply and demand curves, this is shown in Figure 10 and discussed in Box 3, but these can safely be omitted by readers who prefer words to

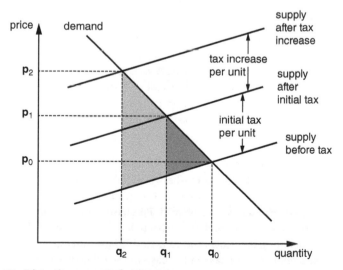

10. **Distortionary cost of a sales tax.**

Box 3 Distortionary cost of a sales tax: interpretation of Figure 10

The diagram illustrates the distortionary cost of a per-unit sales tax imposed on a single good. It is a 'partial equilibrium' analysis—i.e. restricted to effects in the market concerned, and disregarding effects in markets for other goods and for labour and other factors of production.

Following the imposition of the tax, the quantity sold falls from q_0 to q_1. The economic cost of this distortion arises because some sales are no longer made that could have been made profitably before the tax. The size of the economic loss associated with each forgone sale is the difference between the price at which the seller would have been willing to sell, as shown by the supply schedule, and the price which the buyer would have been willing to pay, as shown by the demand schedule. The area of the dark-shaded triangle measures the total loss across all the forgone sales. It corresponds to the sum of forgone producer surplus and consumer surplus on these sales.

If the tax rate per unit is doubled, the quantity sold falls to q_2. With the linear demand and supply schedules shown here, the additional fall in sales is the same as when the initial tax was imposed, but the additional distortionary cost, shown with the pale shading, is much greater than the initial distortionary cost. The *marginal* excess burden is higher than the *average* excess burden.

pictures). The effect of the tax is to open up a difference—equal to the rate of the tax per unit—between the price that the seller of the product receives for each unit sold, and the price that the buyer pays for each unit consumed. Purchasers make their decisions about how much they wish to buy on the basis of the price including tax while producers decide how much to produce and offer for sale on the basis of the price they receive after the tax is deducted. This difference means that there are some sales that would be made if no tax was charged that are no longer made if tax has to be paid. These forgone sales involve an economic loss equal to the gain that would otherwise have been made from the trade.

Suppose, for example, someone is considering whether to engage a decorator to paint their house, and has decided that they would be willing to pay up to €1,000 for this, but at a higher price than this they would prefer to save their money for other purposes. If the minimum price that a decorator needs to charge in order for the work to be profitable is €900, then, in the absence of tax, there is a price at which the buyer and seller can agree: in this case, a price somewhere between €900 and €1,000. There is a net gain of €100 from the trade between the buyer and the seller: the householder has work done for which they would be willing to pay €1,000, while the decorator does work that would have been worthwhile at any price above €900. (How this €100 gain is shared between the buyer and seller depends on the price they agree, but this does not affect the present analysis). However, if the decorator is required to charge tax on their bill at 20 per cent, the minimum price that they would need to charge, while still receiving a net amount sufficient to make the job worthwhile, is €1,080. There is now no price on which the householder and the decorator could agree; the minimum the decorator needs to charge, including the tax, is more than the maximum the householder is willing to pay. The tax has 'distorted' their negotiations so that a potentially profitable transaction is no longer worthwhile, and it has led to an economic loss—a 'distortionary cost'—in the form of the €100 benefit that the two parties would otherwise have shared.

Charging tax on a particular good or service has economic costs which are the forgone gains from trades which no longer take place. These distortionary costs will depend on the size of the tax that is charged, and on the impact of the tax on buyer and seller behaviour. The higher price that buyers face as a result of the tax will reduce the amount they wish to purchase; the lower price that sellers receive, after tax, will reduce the amount they can profitably supply. For a given level of tax, the greater the impact of the tax on the quantity of trade, the greater the economic cost, in terms of the forgone economic benefit from these trades. These changes in demand and supply are generally summarized in the notion of the elasticity of demand and supply—in other words, the responsiveness of demand and supply to changes in price. The distortionary cost of taxation will be higher, for a given tax rate, the more elastic are demand and supply: in other words, the more buyers and sellers respond to changes in price.

Optimal commodity taxation

Excess burden from any tax varies with the tax rate and with the characteristics of the market where the tax is imposed. Other things being equal, higher tax rates are associated with very much higher excess burdens. Roughly speaking, excess burden tends to rise with the square of the tax rate, so that doubling a tax rate increases the excess burden by a factor of four. Excess burdens also depend on the characteristics of the market. The distortionary cost of taxation is higher in more price-sensitive markets, where either demand or supply or both are significantly reduced by higher taxes.

Taken together, these two arguments create a case for taxation which is broadly based (to avoid excessively high tax rates on any individual tax base), but which is also differentiated to take account of market characteristics. In the early 1930s the economist and mathematician Frank Ramsey published one of the classic results in the economics of taxation, in which he showed that a government with a fixed revenue requirement which it had to meet by levying sales taxes would minimize the overall excess burden by setting different rates of tax on different goods and services. In broad terms, Ramsey proposed an 'inverse elasticity' rule for commodity tax rates. Goods and services should be taxed at rates which are set in inverse proportion to the elasticities of demand and supply. In other words, products where a given tax rate leads to large changes in the amounts bought and sold should be taxed at lower rates than products where the same tax rate would have little effect on the quantity traded.

Ramsey's ground-breaking work sparked a new field of economic research: the theory of optimal taxation. This extensive literature asks the question: What pattern of taxes should be employed, in order to achieve a given revenue requirement at least economic cost? Subsequently, the literature developed to ask a more complex question: What pattern of taxes should be employed to achieve a desired balance between efficient revenue-raising and fairness in the distribution of the tax burden?

It turns out that Ramsey's original result, recommending that sales taxes should vary across goods, is actually quite fragile, and depends critically on the range of tax instruments that are available. In particular, if income can be taxed as well as spending, the case for setting different tax rates on different goods and services is substantially weaker. Economists have tended, therefore, to turn towards favouring uniform sales taxes, with the same rate of tax applied to all goods and services. This has substantial practical advantages, since it makes sales tax administration much simpler. In a country that has a well-developed system of income taxation, the economic benefit from differentiating taxes on goods and services may be small relative to the administrative complications that are caused by setting different tax rates.

The case for taxing land

Most of the taxes that governments use to raise revenue involve some distortionary impact on market behaviour. Income taxes, payroll taxes, sales taxes such as VAT, and corporate profits taxes all affect economic behaviour in various different ways. All impose economic costs in the course of revenue-raising to a greater or lesser degree. If we recognize this, then tax policy becomes a matter of compromise: of finding the pattern of taxes that raises the required revenues while causing the least-costly disturbance to economic activity. Since the economic cost of raising revenue from any individual tax tends to rise more than in proportion to the tax rate, a tax system that aims to minimize the overall economic cost of raising revenues would spread the burden of revenue-raising over a number of different taxes, using each tax to the extent that it can raise revenues more cheaply than the other taxes available. If the marginal excess burden differs between taxes, the overall costs of raising revenue could be reduced by making greater use of taxes with lower distortionary costs. In the most efficient portfolio of taxes, each tax will be used up to the point where the marginal excess burden incurred in raising an additional pound in revenue is the same across all taxes.

Two possible tax instruments, however, involve no distortionary cost in raising revenues: a poll tax and a tax on land values.

A poll tax takes the form of a fixed amount per head of population. Since this is not based on anything that the taxpayer can alter, it collects revenue without distorting taxpayer behaviour. The taxpayer is made worse off by the amount of the tax, but by no more than this.

It is, however, easy to see why very little use is made of poll taxes in actual practice. For a poll tax to collect revenues without distorting individual behaviour, it has to be unaffected by decisions that the individual can make. No account can be taken of the taxpayer's income: the tax must be applied in full regardless of whether the taxpayer is rich or poor. Throughout history, the imposition of a poll tax has provoked opposition because of its fundamental unfairness and the heavy tax burden that it imposes on the poor, without regard to their ability to pay (Figure 11). Also, as a purely practical matter, if the tax is to be feasible and yet collected at the same rate from rich and poor, it must realistically be set at a very low level. The revenue-raising power of most other

11. Taxation without fairness. Public protests against the 'Community Charge', a poll tax introduced in 1990 to finance local government in the UK. The tax was abolished in 1993.

taxes is substantially greater, because the amount charged varies directly or indirectly with each taxpayer's ability to pay.

The key characteristic that enables a poll tax to raise revenues without incurring economic costs is that it is a *fixed* amount for each person, and not necessarily that it should be the *same* amount per person. What is crucial is that the amount paid by each person is not influenced by any decision they can make. A tax that was completely random, or that varied according to some unalterable physical characteristic of individuals such as height or eye colour, would doubtless be seen as grotesquely unfair, but would involve no distortionary cost. Some unlucky taxpayers would pay more than others, but there would be nothing they could do to alter this, and therefore no possibility that the tax would distort their decision-making. Likewise—and more seriously—if we think of people being born with certain innate capabilities that may affect their future earning potential, and if we were able to observe these characteristics and levy taxes based on them, then we might be able to levy a tax that was both efficient—since it was based on characteristics that the individual could not change—and more equitable than any other, since we could tax people with higher future earning potential more heavily than those with lower potential. Sadly, however, we cannot observe earnings potential in any reliable way, and so we are stuck with levying taxes on actual earnings, and the distortionary costs that this entails.

Besides a poll tax, one further tax can potentially raise revenues without incurring a distortionary cost. In the late 19th century the US radical writer and political thinker Henry George came to prominence, advocating a tax on land values as the sole basis for financing government. George argued his case from many different angles, pointing out, for example, that the high value of land in downtown Manhattan was not created by its owner, but by its location and by the economic activity that surrounds it. Landowners do not earn the rents they receive as a result of their labour and effort; instead, they are passive recipients of value created by others.

The core of George's argument is that the taxation of land, unlike other taxes, does not jeopardize productive activity; it merely means that some of the rent which would accrue to landowners accrues to the government instead. We can see why this should be so, by looking back to our earlier discussion of the distortionary costs of taxation. There we saw that the distortionary cost of taxation related to the elasticities of demand and supply for the taxed good. If either demand or supply is completely inelastic, a tax will not affect the quantity sold, and the good can be taxed without distortion. Since land is in fixed supply, a tax on land will not affect the quantity of land which is used—at least, until the tax reaches a level that exceeds its economic value, in other words the rent that would have been paid on it. Rents accruing to landowners could in principle be fully taxed, without imposing any distortionary cost at all.

The logic of this part of George's argument is impeccable. So why do we not make far more use of land taxation as the basis for financing the activities of government? The answer seems likely to lie in two very different reasons. First, there is a simple story of political power and influence; the voice of landowners may well be heard much more clearly in government circles than the arguments of campaigners and pamphleteers such as Henry George, or of academic economists for that matter. Second, and probably much more decisively, it is one thing to say that a high level of taxation could be imposed on land on a continuing basis without incurring costs of economic distortion, and another to say that it could be *introduced* without harm. The value of land to its owner and to any potential purchaser is the stream of future benefits that can be derived from its ownership. If the rents that could be earned from land ownership will in the future accrue to the government in taxation, the value of land will drop sharply, by the full capitalized amount of all present and future expected taxes. In other words, a change in tax policy towards land would have its full effect on the current owners of land, who would find themselves in possession of an asset whose value had dropped drastically.

The effect of changes in land taxation illustrates the more general principle that we saw earlier, that change in the taxation of assets will be liable to cause substantial changes in asset values, capitalizing the present and future value of the tax change. Whatever the attraction of changing the tax treatment of physical or financial assets, governments need to be wary of the turmoil in asset values that they could cause by changing asset taxation, and by the substantial capital losses that could be incurred by those who happen to be the current owners.

Taxes and the labour market

We have left until last the issue of the economic impact of taxes in the labour market—the distortionary and disincentive effects of taxes on work. The labour market is potentially the area where tax policy is likely to involve the most significant economic costs, both because such large revenues are raised from taxes explicitly imposed on employment income (income tax and social insurance contributions), and also because a significant part of the burden of other taxes—in particular, taxes levied on the sale of goods and services—may be borne by employees, in a way that also affects labour market incentives and behaviour.

We can think about the economic costs associated with taxes on labour income using much the same framework as we used earlier in this chapter to analyse the economic cost of imposing a tax on the sale of a single good. As in that case, a tax on labour will have effects which are governed by behaviour on both sides of the market, in other words, by the interaction of demand and supply. In the labour market, this is a matter of the interaction between the labour demand of employers, and the labour supply of individuals.

As far as labour demand is concerned—the amount of employment that firms are willing to offer at a given wage rate—the effect of taxes on payroll and labour income is straightforward. If the employer has to pay more in tax on their wage bill, this increases the total labour cost of employing each worker, and the demand for labour will fall. Some production that would be profitable when labour costs are low becomes unprofitable when labour costs are higher.

The impact of income tax is more complicated when we look at the other side of the labour market and consider labour supply, the decisions that individuals make about whether and how much to work. These decisions are more complex in themselves, and are affected by taxes in a more complex way. Let us begin by looking at what is the more straightforward case, the choice 'at the margin', made by someone deciding whether to work an extra hour or not. Subsequently, we will need to consider 'non-marginal' choices—the decision whether to work at all.

Suppose someone already in employment has the opportunity to choose whether to work an additional hour or not. Perhaps their employer offers them a completely free choice about the number of hours they work, or perhaps they are being offered an hour of overtime. Their decision whether to work the extra hour will reflect a range of financial and non-financial consequences, which will be weighed up in different ways by different individuals. Their decision will reflect the possible inconvenience and costs of one more hour's work (additional child care costs and complications, less time to prepare meals and for other housework, less leisure time...). It will also reflect their enjoyment or otherwise of work. Is an extra hour of work interesting and rewarding, or is it an additional hour of tedium and drudgery? Finally we would expect it to be influenced by the financial consequences—the additional money they would earn. It is here that taxes come into the story—in two ways. First, because income tax reduces the wage they receive; their net wage after tax is lower than the gross wage paid by their employer. Second, because sales taxes reduce the purchasing power of each pound they earn, and hence reduce the quantity of goods and services they can buy as a result of the extra hour's work. For the moment we will leave this issue to one side and maintain our focus on taxes on labour income alone, but we return to sales taxes later.

Although we often refer to the 'disincentive' effects of income taxes, it will be seen that the effect of income tax is not always in the direction of reducing the amount that an individual chooses to work. A tax on labour income has, in fact, two different effects, which economists refer to as the 'substitution' and 'income' effects, respectively, and these do not necessarily pull in the same direction.

The substitution effect arises because—for a given standard of living—a tax on labour income affects the attractiveness of work at the margin. In other words, it reduces the gain from an additional hour's work, compared with the alternative—more time for leisure, perhaps. The substitution effect of an income tax certainly works in the direction of reducing labour supply. If an increase in income tax could be implemented in such a way that it did not affect someone's overall standard of living and only impacted on their decision whether to work an extra hour or not, it is clear that additional tax acts as a disincentive. Fewer people would choose to work the extra hour.

But the substitution effect of an income tax is only part of the story. There is a second effect—the income effect—to take into account. Raising the tax on labour income also makes the worker poorer than before by the amount of the additional money taken away in tax from the proceeds of all hours worked, and not just the marginal hour. Generally we would expect this to work in the opposite direction to the substitution effect: a worker who is poorer might decide to work *more*, to make up some of the lost income, sacrificing some non-work time—'leisure time'—in order to maintain their material standard of living. Indeed, if the income effect is sufficiently strong, it is conceivable that it would outweigh the substitution effect, so that the overall effect of higher income tax would be to increase, rather than reduce, the amount that people work. The evidence, however, suggests that in reality income effects are quite modest, reducing the size of the response to taxes, but not changing its direction.

Not all labour supply decisions can be analysed in this marginal framework. Some workers may indeed have a reasonably free choice about precisely how many hours to work, and can make decisions about working hours by considering the costs and benefits of an additional hour's work, at the margin. However, many do not: many jobs offered are for a fixed number of hours, and workers face very little choice over the number of hours they work. Then the decision becomes a 'participation' decision—whether to work or not—rather than a marginal decision about the number of hours of work. And, while the factors that enter into the decision may be much the same, the choice is an all-or-nothing choice, and will be governed by the *total* costs and total benefits from working, and not just the *marginal* net income and other consequences of an extra hour's work.

This is particularly important when we consider how taxes interact with social benefits, such as those paid to the unemployed. Marginal tax rates matter less in people's participation decisions than the overall tax burden on their employment—in other words, the average rate of tax. In addition, for anyone who would qualify for social benefits if they were not working, the level of those benefits will also influence their choices.

Merely identifying the possibility that higher taxes might affect labour supply does not of course demonstrate that taxation has a significant effect on whether and how much people work. Tax policy needs to be based on evidence of the effects of taxes, and how they influence how people actually behave in the real-world labour market.

Fortunately this is an area where major progress has been made in recent years, both in the development of sophisticated research methods and in their application to detailed data for a number of countries. There is now a broad consensus about the scale and pattern of the effects of income taxes on individual employment and working patterns. Overall, and on average, taxes seem to reduce labour supply, but the effects vary widely between different groups in the population.

By and large, the evidence indicates that taxes have very little effect on the labour supply of men and of women who do not have children. Most are employed full-time, and have little opportunity to vary their hours of work.

For low-earners—low-skilled men and women with low earnings potential—there is more evidence that taxes (and social benefits) affect whether or not they are in work, but if they are employed there is not much evidence that taxes influence their hours of work.

Effects of taxes on working patterns are much larger among two groups in the population: women with school-age children, and those over 50. For both these groups, the taxation of earnings seems to reduce work and working hours quite significantly.

Equity and efficiency

To the extent that marginal income tax rates exert a negative effect on employment, income tax policy has to face up to a sharp, and largely unavoidable, trade-off between achieving distributional equity between rich and poor, and minimizing the efficiency costs of taxation, in terms of disincentive effects and other distortions to working behaviour. Tax policies which minimize the distortionary impact of labour income taxation are generally ones which will sharpen inequality in the distribution of income, and make the least contribution to narrowing the gap between rich and poor.

Since the marginal rate of income tax is what (in the main) governs the amount of labour market distortion caused by income taxation, the distortionary impact of taxation will be reduced by levying the lowest possible marginal tax rate for a given revenue requirement.

The trade-off between equity and efficiency can be considered by thinking about a simple income tax system with an initial allowance of tax-free income and a single marginal tax rate applying to all income above this allowance. In an income tax system of this form, the distributional progressivity of the income tax can be increased by increasing the size of the initial tax-free allowance. However, to raise the same revenue as before, the marginal tax rate on income above the allowance then has to be raised. The effect is that greater progressivity—in other words, more equity—comes at the cost of greater distortion—less 'efficiency' in revenue-raising.

Tax policy then involves a compromise between two fundamental objectives—equity and economic efficiency. Where the balance is drawn between the two will depend on the weight that we want to give to distributional equity in tax policy. The greater the weight we want to give to equity, the more we will have to accept a cost in terms of inefficiency and distortion in the labour market. A large tax-free allowance gives greater progressivity but more distortion in the labour market; a smaller tax-free allowance gives less progressivity and requires lower marginal rates, and hence less distortion.

The American economist Arthur Okun summed up this trade-off between equity and efficiency in the memorable image of a leaky bucket. Income can be transferred from rich to poor, but the bucket that is used for this has a leak, which means that some income is lost in the course of the transfer. How large a leak, Okun asked, would we be prepared to tolerate, before deciding that greater economic fairness was just too costly to achieve? Okun suggested that he himself would be willing to tolerate a leakage of no more than 60 cents for each $1 successfully transferred to the poor.

The least distortionary tax, of course, would not be an income tax at all. A poll tax is effectively the extreme version of an income tax in which the marginal tax rate is set to zero, and the tax-free allowance is large and *negative*, so that all taxpayers make a single lump-sum tax payment, irrespective of their level of income. Few commentators—not even the most extreme free-marketeers—would advocate that all taxation should take this non-distortionary form. Even though income-related taxes involve economic costs, fairness in the distribution of the tax burden plays an important role in maintaining social cohesion and public consent. In making tax policy, all decisions realistically involve weighing up the competing claims of equity and efficiency; the major point of political disagreement is about where to draw that balance.

Tax wedges in the labour market

In the previous chapter we saw how taxes on both sides of the labour market would be expected to have the same incidence. Similarly, the overall marginal tax rate on employment income will comprise both the taxes on wages and wage income paid by employers and employees.

A tax on wages or labour income means the cost to the employer of employing a worker for an additional hour's work will be greater than the additional benefit to the employee of the extra hour's wages. This will be true, regardless of whether the tax on wages is levied on the employer or the employee. If the tax is levied on the employer, the total cost of employing the worker for an additional hour will be the wage plus the tax, while the employee will only receive the wage. If the tax is levied on the employee as an income tax, the cost to the employer will be the gross wage, but the benefit to the employee will be the net wage after paying the tax.

We refer to the gap between what the employer pays and what the employee receives as the 'tax wedge' in the labour market, reflecting the idea that the tax drives apart the cost to the employer and the benefit to the employee.

Figure 12 shows the overall marginal tax wedge in some selected OECD countries. Since the tax wedge varies, depending on the level of income, and in some cases the family characteristics of the employee, these are calculated for a particular worker—in this case a single worker without children—in each country for three different income levels, for a worker earning two-thirds of the average wage in the country concerned, the average wage, and two-thirds more than the average wage. Even allowing for the fact that countries differ in terms of their overall level of taxation, countries differ significantly in the marginal tax wedge on employment income, and in how the tax wedge varies across different income levels. In some countries the marginal tax wedge is higher on higher incomes; others show a different pattern.

Uniformity of the marginal tax wedge across different income levels is not necessarily a particular virtue. We saw earlier in this chapter that taxes have a greater effect on the working behaviour of some groups of the workforce than others. It will be particularly important to design tax policies so as to avoid high rates of tax on those whose behaviour is most likely to be sensitive to high marginal tax rates on income: the low-skilled, women with children, and older workers.

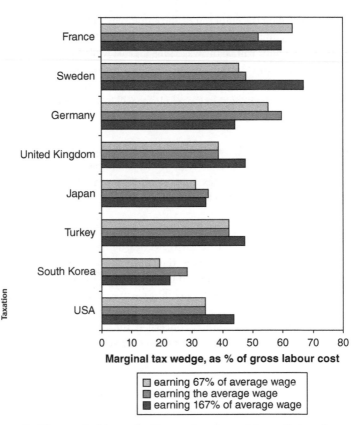

12. **The marginal tax wedge (income tax plus social security taxes) on a single worker, without children, earning different levels of wages, in selected countries, 2010.**

Note: Countries are shown here in descending order of tax as a percentage of GDP in 2012.

Interaction between income tax and benefit policies

Maintaining incentives to work places a tight constraint on tax and benefit policies at the lower end of the income scale. Here it is not just income tax that affects incentives. Indeed, in many countries, workers earning low wages pay very little in income tax. The potential disincentives arise from the combined effects of income tax and the operation of income-related social benefits. Taken together, the additional income tax paid on wages, coupled with the withdrawal of income-related benefits as more is earned, can result in a substantial total rate of deduction from employment income that can be very much higher than the rates of tax paid by the rest of the population.

For example, most countries have some form of social insurance or public assistance paid to someone who is unemployed. An unemployed person who takes a job starts to earn wages, but at the same time loses the entitlement to the unemployment benefits. In extreme cases they could be better off not working, in the sense that the income they earn, once taxed, is less than the level of unemployment benefit. It is not always easy to prevent this situation arising since benefit entitlements often take account of the number of children and other dependants a benefit claimant has to support. If benefits are adequate to provide an acceptable standard of living for large households, it is quite possible that they could exceed the net earnings from low-paid employment. Income tax may exacerbate this problem, but it is often a relatively minor factor in ensuring that people with very low earning power are able to benefit financially from employment.

Recent OECD estimates of the 'participation tax rate'—in other words, the total of income tax and benefit losses—faced by a low-paid worker taking a job after a long period of unemployment are often much higher than the marginal income tax rates faced by most of the population. In the UK, France, and Germany this 'participation tax rate' lies between 60 per cent and 80 per cent of the wage that such a worker would receive. Only about one-third of this is accounted for by income tax and social insurance contributions; the loss of benefits paid to the unemployed is equivalent to an additional tax rate of about 50 per cent on the worker's wages.

This problem can be alleviated by allowing low-paid workers to retain at least some portion of social assistance even when they are in work, relating the payment to the level of the worker's income or the income of their household. Extending entitlement in this way avoids the abrupt withdrawal of benefit entitlement faced by someone who starts work, or whose income rises above some qualifying threshold. Instead, the withdrawal of benefit can be gradually 'tapered', so that the amount paid in benefit falls gradually as income rises. This tapering avoids the massive disincentive effect that arises with abrupt withdrawal. However, it can only do so by spreading a smaller disincentive all the way up the income scale, until the point where entitlement is fully withdrawn. This increases public spending costs, since more households are entitled to some level of assistance, and it means that more people face marginal benefit withdrawal, increasing their marginal rate of effective taxation above the rate of income tax. Whether these consequences are worth the benefits of improving the incentive for unemployed workers to take low-paid jobs will depend on a difficult assessment of how far the working behaviour of people in different circumstances is affected by high rates of effective taxation. There is no easy way out of this dilemma.

Do consumption taxes harm work incentives less?

It is sometimes suggested that damage done to work incentives by high taxes on labour incomes could be reduced by shifting revenue-raising away from income taxes towards consumption taxes such as VAT. Certainly, VAT has considerable revenue-raising potential, and the revenues it raises could give scope for a substantial reduction in income taxes on wages. But the idea that this shift in the pattern of taxation avoids the distortionary effects of taxes in the labour market is simply mistaken. Taxes levied on spending reduce the quantity of goods and services that can be purchased from the proceeds of an additional hour's work in just the same way as a tax on income does.

How much more do consumption taxes add to the burden of tax on labour incomes? In particular, how much do they add to the marginal tax rate? The answer is not straightforward since it depends on how individual consumption patterns change as workers earn additional income. However, figures for 2005 from the OECD indicate that consumption taxes on average added a further 6.7 per cent to the tax wedge on earnings, raising the overall tax wedge in OECD countries from an average of 38.6 per cent to 45.3 per cent. In the UK, where a significant part of consumption is zero-rated for VAT, the tax wedge on earnings is increased from 34 per cent to 39.5 per cent when account is taken of the VAT and excise tax payments on consumption.

While the distortionary impact on the labour market of raising a given amount of revenue through an increase in the marginal rate of income tax and an increase in the rate of VAT may be similar, there are two differences of some significance between income tax and a sales tax such as VAT.

The first is that they affect the interests of different generations differently. Switching from a tax on income to a tax on spending acts to disadvantage older generations relative to younger generations—in particular, the retired who have saved out of taxed income face an increased tax burden on their spending, while for younger generations the tax change makes little difference.

The second difference arises when the income tax has a progressive distributional incidence—for example, when the income tax schedule begins with a significant allowance of tax-free income. As a result, the marginal rate of income tax (which governs the amount of distortion) tends to be much higher than the average rate of income tax (which determines the amount of revenue raised). Sales taxes, by contrast, tend to apply to all consumption and imply rather lower marginal rates for a given amount of revenue. As a result, an equal-revenue switch from income tax to VAT *can* reduce the overall *marginal* tax wedge on earnings. However, it does so only because the tax on spending is less progressive than the income tax, and therefore marginal tax rates are lower. Proposals to shift from income tax to VAT only achieve a reduction in the overall marginal tax wedge by making the tax system less redistributive, a feature that is rarely stated explicitly by those advocating such a tax shift.

Chapter 5
Tax evasion and enforcement

Effective tax policy is not simply a matter of deciding on the taxes that people should pay, but also of ensuring that they actually do pay what they should. The practical operation and enforcement of the tax system is every bit as important as the structure and rates of tax in ensuring that revenues are raised efficiently and fairly. To a significant extent, good tax compliance is what distinguishes well-functioning states from chaotic and ineffective ones. Greece and Germany, for example, employ many of the same taxes. The most significant difference in the functioning of their tax system is the extent of evasion.

This chapter will look at tax evasion from three perspectives. First, from the taxpayer perspective: How and why do people evade taxes? Second, from the perspective of the economy: How can we assess the amount of revenue lost through evasion? Third, from the perspective of the revenue authorities: How can tax evasion be controlled?

Individual tax evasion

Oliver Wendell Holmes Jr, a distinguished Justice of the US Supreme Court, famously wrote in a letter to the British politician Harold Laski, 'I pay my tax bills more readily than any others—for whether the money is well-spent or ill-spent I get civilized society for it.' One only has to make the most cursory searches of the internet to find many who do not share Holmes's enthusiasm for paying taxes, and who express their indignation about taxation in the most forthright terms. And even if many taxpayers did share Holmes's view that taxation is the price that ensures a civilized society, there might well be many who would rather that others paid the price, and who would be tempted to minimize their own tax bill.

How do the temptations arise, and what determines who succumbs to them?

Three broad factors seem to play a role in determining how many people seek to evade tax, and how much tax they manage to keep out of the hands of the revenue authorities. First, and probably most important, are the opportunities that people face to influence the tax that they pay. Many tax systems operate in a way that leave the majority of taxpayers with little scope to evade tax. The tax due on their income is withheld at source by their employer, or by the bank that pays them interest, and they never get their hands on it. In cases where taxpayers do have control over their tax payments, the extent to which they declare their full earnings and pay all the tax that they should will be influenced by two further groups of factors: their perception of the gains and risks involved; and a complex mix of moral, psychological, and social pressures.

Opportunities for evasion

Most tax evasion takes place in a context where taxpayers—individuals or firms—are required to report income or spending to the tax authorities. Often this takes the form of an annual tax return, which has to be completed with details of relevant income or sales during the preceding year together with other information relevant to their tax liability, and filed (submitted) by a particular deadline.

The opportunities for tax evasion principally arise through the scope to make false or incomplete statements in the tax return without prompting a successful challenge by the revenue authorities. This can be a matter of simple under-declaration: the taxpayer declares a lower income than they actually received, or for a sales tax, a lower level of sales. Alternatively, an individual can try to reduce their tax liability by false or exaggerated claims for deductions or allowances against tax. If an income tax system allows the cost of donations to charity to be deducted from gross income, before tax is computed, then a taxpayer may try to reduce their tax payment by exaggerating the amount of money they have donated to charitable causes. If the cost of mortgage interest, children's schooling, or commuting expenses can be offset against income tax, taxpayers can claim a higher level of costs than they have in fact incurred. In each case, however, the basic sequence of events is the same: the taxpayer provides misleading information which would reduce their liability to tax, and keeps their fingers crossed that the revenue authorities cannot spot the lie.

More rarely in most developed countries, tax evasion can take the form of completely hidden activity which lies entirely out of view of the revenue authorities. It may be possible for individuals to work or to trade as a business without the revenue authorities being aware of their existence at all—so-called 'ghosts', in the jargon used by some tax authorities. However, most individuals with full-time employment or business activities are unlikely to be able to conceal their existence from the revenue authorities for any length of time, and the majority of ghosts are likely to be working on the margins of the economy, with low working hours and incomes, and consequently rather little tax would be due in any case.

Not all taxes offer equal opportunities for evasion to every individual taxpayer. The scope for income under-declaration by employees is often very limited indeed. Many tax systems require

13. US IRS staff processing income tax returns in 1986. Rapid advances in computing and information technology over the past fifty years have transformed tax administration and opened up opportunities for more effective enforcement.

employers to report the amount of income they have paid in wages to each individual employee, and the authorities can use this information to cross-check the figures that the taxpayer puts in their tax return (Figure 13).

Indeed, many tax systems go further and require the employer to withhold tax from wage payments, and to remit this directly to the revenue authorities. Except in very small firms, long-term collusion between employers and employees to make coordinated false reports of wage payments is unlikely—it would only require one disaffected employee to 'blow the whistle' on such an arrangement. The opportunities for employees to evade tax on their wage income are then limited to making exaggerated claims for deductions and allowances, and the scope for this may also be limited if the tax system confines deductions to those where there is scope for independent reporting and verification.

Many countries also use systems of reporting to cross-check taxpayer declarations of investment incomes—bank interest, etc. Often, the only scope that taxpayers have to evade tax on investment income is to hide their investments abroad, beyond the scope of direct surveillance by the tax authorities. But such arrangements can come dramatically unstuck if information comes into the possession of the revenue authorities. Recently a number of European countries have been offered computer disks containing details of their taxpayers who hold undeclared accounts in Liechtenstein and Swiss financial institutions. Using this data windfall, some European countries have been vigorously investigating and prosecuting evaders.

By contrast, nearly all tax systems are much more exposed to tax evasion by the self-employed—people working on their own account, or the owners of small unincorporated businesses. Part of the reason for this is that the self-employed are in much greater control of the information to be reported; they do not have an employer who may separately report their income to the authorities. In addition the definition of income for the self-employed is more complex and far less clear-cut than for employees, requiring an element of judgement about which different people could reasonably reach different views. Since the boundary between true and false income is imprecise, self-employed taxpayers have scope to exploit the ambiguity.

For example, most tax systems allow people working in a self-employed capacity to deduct from their gross income the costs of the equipment and materials they have used in the course of their business activity, and an individual's tax liability can be reduced by exaggerating these costs. The boundary between the costs of a business and the individual's own consumption can be very blurred indeed. For example, when someone runs a business from home, how much of the cost of their home, their furniture, their telephone bill, their car, and other spending should count as part of the cost of the business? When the boundary is blurred in this way, there is probably a long way that taxpayers can push things, before the revenue authorities can seriously challenge the judgements they are making.

With sales taxes such as VAT, there are a number of different ways in which tax can be evaded. Sales can be under-reported, and this can be backed up by a false set of accounts to show the tax authorities. In a system with multiple rates of tax applying to different categories of goods and services, it may also be possible to reduce the firm's tax bill by exaggerating the proportion of sales which are of products subject to lower tax rates. In a VAT system, moreover, the tax due on the firm's sales is reduced by the amount of the tax paid on the goods and services the firm has purchased, and the firm's tax bill can therefore be reduced by exaggerating the level of the firm's taxed purchases. Most revenue authorities are, of course, wise to this, and would query a business that claimed excessive purchases in relation to its sales, so there is an upper limit to how much the firm can reduce its tax bill in this way, but some scope certainly exists.

Sales tax evasion, backed up by fraudulent accounting, is likely to be most prevalent in smaller firms where financial matters are held under tight individual control by a single individual owner. In larger firms there are greater risks to concealing sales through false accounting because employees have to be involved in the fraud, and this brings additional dangers for the firm. The tricks that are needed to conceal business income from the tax authorities can also be used by employees to enrich themselves at the expense of their employer, and few large firms are likely to want to risk losing financial control in this way.

Some smaller firms may be able to hide from the VAT authorities entirely—the VAT counterpart of income tax 'ghosts'. However, the way VAT works tends to discourage this, at least amongst businesses which act as suppliers to firms that are themselves VAT taxpayers. Since businesses which pay VAT can, in effect, claim back the VAT on any purchase that they make, they will not benefit from purchasing from a supplier who will not charge them VAT, and if they buy untaxed supplies they may well face awkward questions when they come to do their own tax accounts. It is overstating matters to say—as some early proponents of VAT did—that VAT is therefore a self-enforcing tax. However, this feature of the tax does mean that VAT 'ghosts' are likely to be small-scale operations, predominantly selling to private customers rather than to other businesses. In countries like the UK where firms only pay VAT when their turnover exceeds a moderately high annual threshold (currently about £85,000) the amount of tax revenue lost from such small-scale VAT ghosts may well be rather small.

A much larger source of VAT revenue loss through fraud and evasion has attracted a lot of attention in recent years. European countries' VAT systems refund VAT on goods which are exported, and large-scale criminal frauds have been able to exploit this arrangement to milk the VAT system of billions of euros, by creating a merry-go-round of artificial transactions, in which goods are repeatedly exported and imported, with a claim for VAT refund being made each time the goods are exported. These frauds have been particularly alarming because they are potentially unlimited. Unlike income tax fraud and evasion, which, at worst, could drive tax revenues down to zero, these export-refund VAT frauds work by 'reclaiming' tax which was in fact never paid in the first place, which means that, if unchecked, they could drive VAT revenue down beyond zero. Fortunately, measures taken in response to these frauds seem to have checked their growth, for the time being at least.

With corporation taxes, revenue losses through outright fraud and evasion are probably less significant than two distinctive categories of revenue loss. Both of these come under the heading of tax avoidance rather than evasion. While tax evasion is clearly illegal, avoidance is less easily defined. It involves organizing the

81

taxpayer's affairs, within the boundaries set by the ruling tax legislation, so as to minimize the taxpayer's tax liability. In principle, therefore, it lies wholly within the letter of the law—if not the spirit, since much avoidance exploits contrived situations, undertaken with the primary purpose of avoiding tax.

Substantial corporate tax revenues are lost through the aggressive exploitation of loopholes, blurred boundaries, and ambiguities in the tax system and in the formulation of tax legislation, backed up by a willingness to devote substantial resources to legal action. Businesses that engage in aggressive tax planning of this sort can often make a huge return on the resources they invest in fighting legal cases, and they know that in many cases the tax authorities will be unable or reluctant to match their legal weaponry. The problem for society is that such battles are wasteful of potentially productive resources. Instead, lawyers have to be engaged, not in producing something of real value, but in shifting, or contesting the shifting, of resources from the public sector to the pockets of firms. Tax authorities have to make a difficult judgement of how much public money to devote to fighting such cases, when there are easier, and less wasteful, ways of raising additional revenues. Undoubtedly, the world would be a better place without aggressive tax planning and speculative litigation, but since these activities are essentially legal, it is difficult to see how they can be prevented. It can help if tax legislation is clear and leaves few loopholes to exploit, but this is easier said than done.

Massive revenues, too, are lost through international corporate tax avoidance. Multinational companies have opportunities to structure themselves in a way that minimizes their liability to taxes in countries where they conduct their business, and instead to shift the profits they earn to lower taxed jurisdictions and tax havens where they may pay no tax at all. Profits can be shifted through a number of mechanisms, in particular through transfer pricing—manipulation of the prices at which the business charges its internal transactions between subsidiaries in different countries—and through charges for the use of the business's intellectual property—rights, patents, and the like. In both cases, a business unit in a high-tax country can be charged high prices for these internal transactions, reducing the profits earned in the high-tax country, and enabling the profits to be relocated elsewhere in the organization, in places where they will be taxed less.

Individual risks and gains from evasion

What determines whether an individual taxpayer decides to evade tax, given the opportunity, and by how much? Some insights can be obtained from a simple economic framework, in which individuals decide whether to evade tax, and how much tax to evade, based on a comparison of costs and benefits—weighing up, on the one hand, the gains from evasion in terms of unpaid tax, and, on the other hand, the risks of being caught and penalized.

In the simplest version of this economic model, an individual might face an opportunity to be honest or dishonest about the receipt of a particular one-off payment—for example, a one-off payment of £1,000. In the absence of any moral considerations, the individual might weigh up the consequences of dishonesty, which amount to the tax saving they would make if they were successful in evading tax, and, if they were unsuccessful, the penalty they would face. If we suppose the tax rate to be 20 per cent, and the penalty for evasion to be twice the level of the tax, plus payment of the tax due, then evasion offers a benefit to the individual in the form of a tax saving of £200 if they are undetected, and a cost of £400 if they are caught and fined. In both cases these amounts are measured against the alternative, which is honestly paying the tax that is due. It will be clear that a crucial element in the calculation of the consequences of evasion will be an assessment of the risk of being detected and punished. If the probability of detection is sufficiently high, the potential evader may think that the potential tax saving is not worth the risks involved.

In the example, if the individual reckons the risk of getting caught is 1 in 3 or higher, then on average there is no net gain from evasion. For example, if half of all evaders are caught, then they face a 50/50 chance of getting away with the evasion, in which case they save £200 in tax, but a 50/50 chance of being found out, in which case they have to pay the tax due, plus a fine twice as high as the tax saving they would have made. In this case, evasion clearly is not worthwhile. If the risk of being caught is exactly 1 in 3, then they have to weigh up a 1 in 3 chance of losing £400, compared to a 2 in 3 chance of gaining £200. For an individual who did not care about the riskiness of the outcome, this level of risk would be exactly the tipping-point between compliance and evasion; with a greater risk of detection they would comply, but with a smaller risk of detection they would evade, because on average (averaging over good and bad outcomes, taking into account their probabilities) they would then expect to gain from evasion.

But people who are 'risk-averse'—in other words, who prefer a guaranteed level of income, compared with unpredictable income that has on average the same level—would choose the certainty of compliance against the uncertain outcome from evasion. The more risk-averse someone is, the lower the risk of detection would need to be before they would decide to evade, because they would only contemplate the risky outcome if on average the pay-off from evasion was substantially higher than from law-abiding compliance.

Once we depart from this simple framework of one-off evasion with a fixed amount of tax at stake the analysis becomes more complicated. For example, individuals might have a range of evasion options, and not just a simple yes/no decision to make. They could, for example, have a choice to try to evade part but not all of the tax due, and they might prefer this option if they are uncomfortable about very risky outcomes, but are willing to accept some lower level of risk. Their decision might also be influenced by their judgement of how the risk of being caught was affected by the amount of tax evaded. They might, for example, suspect that it would be harder to conceal a very large level of undeclared income than a more moderate amount. Their decision might also be influenced by how the penalty levied on those who are caught varies with the scale of the fraud. If the penalty is much the same regardless of the amount of tax evaded, we might expect to see very few small-scale evaders, while penalties that rise sharply with the amount of tax at stake might make small-scale evasion less risky than large-scale evasion.

Further complications arise where taxpayers have the opportunity for regular, ongoing evasion, rather than making a decision about a one-off evasion opportunity. The taxpayer's decision about evasion in any particular year might then take into account not just the risk of detection and penalty in that year, but also the longer term consequences of being caught evading tax. If the tax authorities are known to pay more attention to people with a record of evading tax, then the implicit penalty for being caught may be considerably higher than the fine levied, as being caught may also reduce the scope for future undetected evasion.

Some of the features of this analysis can help the revenue authorities design effective strategies for tax enforcement, as we will see later. But the basic story that is told in this economic model—that taxpayers make evasion decisions by weighing up the gains from evasion against the risks of detection and the punishments that would then be imposed—does not satisfactorily account for the level of tax evasion that actually takes place. In most industrialized countries the percentage of taxpayers who are subject to audit—investigation for possible evasion—in any year is often really rather low, and the penalties for evasion are often relatively modest. People who have evaded relatively small amounts of tax may not even face criminal prosecution, and in many cases are charged an administrative penalty which is a relatively small multiple of the tax due. If the only reason that individuals comply is fear of detection and the penalty that would be levied, then the actual rates of investigation and penalties are insufficient to explain what appear to be relatively high levels of tax compliance across the population as a whole. Why do so many people pay their taxes, when the risks of non-compliance are so small?

One possible answer is that many taxpayers are very risk-averse and prefer the certainty of tax compliance against the risky gamble of evasion. But this answer is at odds with the general pattern we see of behaviour in relation to other risky activities, ranging from entrepreneurial investment to participating in risky activities such as skiing. Most people are risk-averse, but not sufficiently risk-averse to explain high tax compliance.

Another explanation could be that taxpayers simply overestimate the risks involved in tax evasion. They may believe that the tax authorities are more all-seeing than they actually are, or that the punishments for evasion are much more drastic. There may be an element of truth in this, but it seems unlikely that the scale of misperception needed to explain observed levels of compliance could last for long. People would surely learn that the risks of evasion were low from their own experience, and from that of friends and neighbours. So, if not risk-aversion or misperception, what can explain the sustained and relatively high levels of tax compliance observed in practice?

We have already seen one part of the answer: many countries' tax systems make extensive use of withholding-at-source—such as the UK's PAYE systems, in which taxes on employment incomes are collected directly from the employer. Elsewhere, payments of wages or bank interest may be reported to the tax authorities, which may make it difficult for the taxpayer to under-declare income without immediately being found out. Relatively few taxpayers may actually have much scope to evade tax, and it is only for these taxpayers that the chance of detection and penalties will be relevant. Moreover, if scope for evasion is confined to relatively small groups of taxpayers—such as the self-employed—the authorities can concentrate their limited resources on auditing these taxpayers much more frequently and intensively.

Another possible explanation for a high level of tax compliance is that there are significant moral and psychological elements in tax evasion decisions. Some taxpayers may comply, not because they fear detection and punishment, but through a sense of moral obligation or 'civic duty', while others may comply because they care about their reputation in the community, or their own self-image. Some have argued that these social and psychological influences are as important in understanding actual taxpayer behaviour as the opportunistic calculation of evasion risks and rewards.

Moral, psychological, and social influences

'If you are not happy with how the government spends your taxes it's OK to hold some of it back by not declaring everything you earn.' A study commissioned for the Australian Tax Office in 1998 asked people to say whether they agreed or disagreed with this statement, and a remarkable 95 per cent disagreed. Few survey questions attract such a uniform response. In this study, as in many others which have posed a variety of questions about tax evasion, in many different countries, there is clearly a significant moral element to tax compliance. The proportion of the population accepting some form of moral obligation to pay taxes varies depending on the precise form of the question posed. The question above seems to have attracted a particularly negative response, perhaps as much because it implied that individuals have the right to pick and choose in their acceptance of the legitimate spending choices of elected governments as because of concerns about tax evasion. But even when faced with a less loaded question, a significant proportion of the population reject evasion as wrong. The 'World Values Survey', conducted periodically across many countries, has asked people to comment on tax evasion, for example asking them to consider 'Cheating on tax if you have the chance', and to rate how far they think this would be justified (Figure 14). Work by Benno Torgler shows that in most European countries about half of all respondents say that such cheating is 'never justified', and tax morality appears to be even stronger in Asian countries, with around 80 per cent of respondents taking this view in Japan, China, and India.

In many cases, the moral view that people themselves take on such questions seems to contrast with a more jaundiced view about the behaviour or attitudes of other people. The psychologist Michael Wenzel points out that in the Australian Tax Office study around half of respondents thought that 'Most people try and avoid paying their fair share of tax'. Similarly, almost half of respondents agreed that 'A lot of people I know think it's OK not to pay tax on cash earnings', but only 8 per cent would admit that this was a view that they themselves held. It is possible, of course, that people are unwilling to own up to having anti-social views themselves, but feel less inhibition when talking about the views of others. A similar phenomenon is sometimes found, for example,

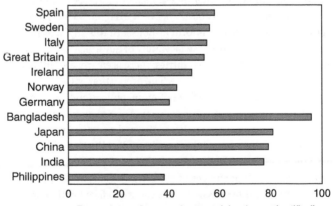

14. 'Cheating on tax if you have the chance. Do you think this is justified?' Answers from the World Values Survey, various years, early/mid-1990s.

in surveys on racist attitudes, and can also bias opinion polls on voting intentions. It is also possible that in answering surveys some people may be wary of giving their own views accurately, for fear that this somehow would be reported back to the authorities. But there does seem a tendency for people to misperceive social norms about tax evasion, and to think that others are less moral, and more actively engaged in evasion than is actually the case.

Research has uncovered some interesting patterns in individual answers to these questions about taxpaying morality. Generally taxpaying morality seems to be higher among older respondents—and sometimes amongst the young—than amongst people of middle age, and it tends to be higher amongst those who are religious and amongst women. It seems to be higher among people who believe that others comply, and to be positively influenced by the perceived quality and efficiency of public services, and the perceived fairness of public policies. Intriguingly there seems to be a tendency for tax morality to be lower among the self-employed. It is not, however, clear whether this is a genuine difference in attitudes, or a self-justification for a group of people who are much more extensively engaged in evasion than many employees.

How much tax is lost through evasion?

People's willingness to evade tax is almost certainly affected by their perception that other people do so and get away with it. Given this, it is perhaps unsurprising that estimates of the extent of tax evasion attract so much attention.

The amount of tax revenue lost through evasion is very uncertain. Reliable estimates are hard to obtain, because taxpayers who go to considerable lengths to conceal their activities from the authorities may also be reluctant to reveal their activities to researchers. Nevertheless, it is important to learn what we can about the level and pattern of evasion, as this is likely to affect the design of public policies, and, in particular, the more effective targeting of the tax authorities' limited resources for audit and investigation.

One approach to investigating the scale and pattern of evasion is to undertake an intensive investigation of a representative sample of taxpayer returns. This approach has a number of merits. It starts from taxpayers' returns, and therefore provides a direct measurement of the level and pattern of under-reporting, and detailed data about how under-reporting relates to taxpayer characteristics. Unfortunately, it can only place a lower bound on evasion, rather than giving a precise estimate, because some under-reporting and evasion may not be uncovered by even the most intensive audit.

Only a few countries have undertaken this sort of intensive investigation and audit of a representative sample of taxpayers. The most extensive investigations have been in the United States, in the form of the Taxpayer Compliance Measurement Program (TCMP), under which the US Internal Revenue Service audited in depth a sample of tax returns roughly every three years from 1963 to 1988. Following concerns about the intrusive nature and cost of the TCMP audits, a less intensive exercise was instituted in the 1990s, the National Research Program (NRP). Overall, taking the personal and corporate income taxes together, the level of income tax evasion in 2001 was found to be around 16 per cent. For the individual income tax, the rate of evasion through under-declaration was about 9 per cent of the total revenue due, and the evasion percentage for the corporate income tax was 17 per cent. Within the individual income components there was wide variation. Under-reporting of individual wages and salaries was only about 1 per cent: most taxpayers know that their wages are reported to the IRS by their employers. There was more under-reporting of self-employed business income, with less than half the true income reported on average.

A similar contrast between employees and the self-employed was found by a one-off tax enforcement study in 2007 by the Danish tax administration, based on an intensive randomized audit experiment involving around 40,000 individual income taxpayers. Overall, the income under-reporting discovered in the audit was equivalent to less than 2 per cent of taxpayers' net income, and the tax lost through the evasion was some 2.4 per cent of the total tax liability of the taxpayers concerned. Under-reporting of income was, once again, closely related to the amount of information which taxpayers knew the authorities had at their disposal. In the case of employment income independently reported by employers the level of evasion was a mere 0.2 per cent. By contrast, taxpayers were less likely to declare incomes which were not subject to third-party reporting, such as self-employment income; overall about 8 per cent of self-employment income was found to be under-reported.

Audits, however well-resourced and thorough, can only ever give a lower bound to the level of income which is concealed from the tax authorities, and some income may remain hidden despite intensive investigation. It is possible that virtually nothing of significance has escaped the attentions of the auditors; but it is also possible that what has been revealed by the audit is only the tip of a very much larger iceberg. What other clues can we find to the true scale of evasion?

Possible indications can be given by various discrepancies in official statistics or from clues given by other aspects of individual behaviour. Official statistics are likely to be affected to varying degrees by tax evasion, depending on the source of information on which the statistics are based. In particular, we would expect statistics that are based on reports by the taxpayers themselves to be more severely contaminated than those that are based on information from other sources. If it is illegal for a plumber to fail to declare income, but not illegal for their customer to employ the plumber, then the plumber might well conceal their income and turnover from a statistical enquiry as well as from the tax authorities—for fear that the statisticians and tax authorities might compare notes—but there would be no reason for the customer to under-report the amount they have spent on the plumber's services.

The UK tax authorities have been able to make regular and quite plausible assessments of the scale of revenue losses through VAT fraud, evasion, and other sources of revenue shortfall—the so-called 'VAT gap'—by calculating how much revenue *should have been* collected, by applying the appropriate VAT rates to official statistics on the level and pattern of consumer spending, and comparing this with the VAT revenue *actually* collected. This approach is far from straightforward, since complex and detailed adjustments are needed to take account of the timing of tax payments, the VAT charged on sales to the public sector and VAT-exempt financial institutions, and the effect of sales by small firms that are not required to charge VAT. While the results are subject to an appreciable margin of error, this work has been useful in indicating the scale of revenue losses through carousel frauds as well as through more routine forms of evasion, such as the under-reporting of sales, and from revenue losses due to bankruptcy and other factors. Overall the VAT gap in the UK appears to have peaked at somewhere around 13–15 per cent of potential revenue about a decade ago, with organized frauds such as carousel fraud accounting for only about a quarter of the total, but has subsequently been reduced to around 10 per cent. Multi-country studies using a similar approach suggest that the overall rate of VAT revenue losses across the EU as a whole may be similar to this, but that there are wide variations among individual member states.

The UK authorities also estimate the scale of revenue losses for the other major UK taxes, although not all of these estimates have such a clear methodological foundation as with the VAT gap estimates. The shortfall in corporation tax receipts—much of it due to aggressive tax planning and avoidance—is believed to be about the same percentage of theoretical receipts as the VAT gap, while the revenue gaps for income tax and excise duties are believed to be significantly smaller. A substantial part of income tax is collected through deduction at source, which leaves little scope for individual evasion, and excise duties are subject to very close monitoring and control by the revenue authorities; for both these taxes revenue shortfalls are thought to be only about 5 per cent.

Tax enforcement

Tax evasion undoubtedly provokes resentment on the part of law-abiding taxpayers. It leads to inequity in the pattern of tax payments, and, to the extent that the lost revenue has to be recovered through higher taxes elsewhere, it increases the tax burden on the rest of the population. The perception that others are evading tax may increase the likelihood that someone may themselves decide to evade tax. For all of these reasons, maintaining a reasonably high level of tax compliance is crucial to maintaining a 'good equilibrium' in which tax revenues are seen to be distributed reasonably equitably across the population, and in which most taxpayers pay their tax bills. Should significant evasion take hold, there is a serious risk that an economy can slide into a 'bad equilibrium' in which taxpayers believe that others are evading tax on a large scale, and decide that they would be foolish not to follow suit.

How can the revenue authorities best deploy their resources to stop people evading tax, or at least reduce the scale of revenue losses?

The obvious first step is in the design of the tax system and tax processes. Designing the tax system so that taxes can, as much as possible, be withheld at source is the single most effective step that can be taken to reducing tax evasion. Taxes can be withheld at source from employment incomes, from bank interest, for company dividends paid to shareholders, and possibly from other payments too. At the very least this then means that tax evasion requires collusion between two parties who may not entirely have shared interests, and at best—as in the majority of industrialized countries—it ensures that a large proportion of tax revenues is gathered cheaply and predictably, with minimal scope for evasion.

As an alternative to withholding at source, a similar, though less watertight, effect can be achieved if the tax authorities require employers, banks, and others making income payments to individual taxpayers to report these payments to the authorities. Taxpayers then know that the authorities have the ability to identify income under-reporting, and this will encourage the bulk of these incomes to be reported honestly in tax returns.

The authorities can then target their efforts on the remaining streams of tax revenue where withholding at source or third party reporting cannot be used.

Tax investigation and enforcement activities are costly. In the simple economic model of tax enforcement outlined earlier in this chapter, taxpayers make their decisions about evasion based on the potential tax saving, and the risks and costs of being caught. The latter, in turn, depend on two factors that policy can influence—the chance that tax evasion will be detected, and the penalties that an evader faces if caught. Increasing the chance that an individual's tax evasion will be detected will require more resources to be devoted to tax investigation, so that a higher proportion of taxpayers can be audited each year, and to increase the intensity and thoroughness of audits. In this simple framework, a higher rate of detection works by increasing the penalty that an evader might, on average, expect to face. However it can only do so by devoting more resources to audit and investigation, and it might be tempting to think that the same effect could be achieved more directly, and at no additional cost in investigation resources, by increasing the severity of the penalties imposed on those who are caught. This brings us to a familiar dilemma in deterrent law enforcement more generally: since we can achieve a given level of deterrence much more cheaply through higher penalties than through more intensive investigation, surely we should save on investigation resources, and impose the most severe penalties imaginable on the few law-breakers who are caught?

The logic may be right, but the framework is overly simplistic. One restriction on the penalties that can be levied for any offence of tax evasion is the need to keep penalties in proportion to the scale on the evasion. If severe penalties are imposed for the most trivial offences, there is a risk that they can push evaders towards more, rather than less, evasion. They may well judge that they might as well be hung for a sheep as a lamb, and turn their attention to more ambitious evasion, knowing that the penalty would be little higher than that imposed on smaller offences. Another restriction on how far the authorities can rely on the deterrent effect of massive penalties is that higher penalties might be hard to impose. Once penalties are high enough to drive taxpayers into bankruptcy, evaders may be indifferent to a higher penalty. Moreover, a perception that the penalty was out of proportion to the seriousness of the crime might make courts—especially jury courts—unwilling to convict.

Most seriously, tax enforcement that relied only on draconian penalties for the few evaders who are unlucky enough to get caught could adversely change the climate of tax payment and compliance, to the detriment of efficient revenue collection. Many tax authorities try to maintain a non-confrontational relationship with taxpayers, believing that this is more likely to encourage willing compliance by taxpayers. By contrast, harsher regimes, with a less cooperative relationship with taxpayers, can provoke taxpayers into passive resistance, which adds to the costs and reduces the effectiveness of administration and enforcement.

The atmosphere of the tax authorities' interactions with taxpayers matters, but so does public confidence that appropriate effort is being devoted to ensuring that 'other people' pay the taxes they should. There are some straightforward strategies to improving the effectiveness of resources available for investigation. Resources can be targeted to areas where past experience has shown that evasion is concentrated, and detection rates are higher, while maintaining some baseline level of audit in other areas, to ensure that some incentive for compliance is maintained. More creative audit strategies can be designed, which try to reshape the incentives for taxpayers towards a higher level of honest declaration. One approach, for example, can use the fact that taxpayers interact annually with the tax authorities, to enhance the incentives for compliance in any given year. Taxpayers who know that if they are caught they will face more intense audit in future years may be more cautious about evasion in the current year to avoid the burden of more intense future audit, and the loss of possible evasion opportunities in later years.

Nothing succeeds like success, so the saying goes, and in the field of tax enforcement there are good reasons to believe this to be true. We have seen that public attitudes towards tax evasion are heavily influenced by what people believe others are doing, and that people tend to think that others are less moral in matters of taxation than they are themselves. If taxpayers believe that their neighbours are failing to pay their fair share of tax they may be less inclined to comply themselves. Ensuring that taxes are paid, and being seen to do so, are amongst the most important steps that can be taken towards encouraging future tax compliance.

Chapter 6
Issues in tax policy

> There are those who seem to have nothing else to do but to
> suggest modes of taxation to men in office.
>> Conservative Prime Minister Robert Peel, in the House of
>> Commons, 1842

Tax policy can be a political minefield, and an area of real danger
for politicians and—at times—the whole system of government.
Changes in taxation have provoked revolts and rebellions
throughout history, sometimes with dramatic consequences.
The independence of the United States from the British Crown
was sparked by resentment to taxes imposed by London.
Opposition to British rule was built around the slogan 'No
taxation without representation', and the Boston 'Tea Party' of
1773, in which shiploads of heavily taxed tea were dumped by
American protesters, led to repression, military conflict,
and the ultimate defeat of the British. In India, Gandhi's
non-violent opposition to British colonial rule began with a
hugely symbolic 'Salt March' in 1930, in protest against the
heavy duties charged on salt—a cause which united all levels of
Indian society, for the tax was a heavy fiscal burden borne by the
poor as well as the better off. In more recent times, the
long-serving and seemingly unstoppable British prime minister
Margaret Thatcher was unseated as the result of public protests
against a reform in local taxation, which replaced the

long-standing local tax on property values with a fixed tax per head, the 'Community Charge' or, colloquially, 'poll tax'. In this there were echoes of Wat Tyler's Peasants' Revolt of 1381, a violent—but ultimately unsuccessful—protest following the imposition of a poll tax to finance Richard II's wars with France.

Tax reformers have to navigate treacherous waters, and it is not surprising that many politicians exercise great caution, even cynicism, in tax policy. Governments need revenues to fund public services and redistribution, and ambitious governments with grand plans and projects need to find creative ways of increasing the revenues they can raise. The 17th century French king Louis XIV, the 'Sun King', was one of the most ambitious and extravagant of monarchs, and needed massive revenues to finance wars, construction projects—including the elaborate Palace of Versailles—and major institutional reform. His controller-general of finance, Jean-Baptiste Colbert, approached this task pragmatically, seeking to raise the necessary money with the minimum of provocation. His maxim for tax policy is widely quoted: 'The art of taxation consists in so plucking the goose as to obtain the largest possible amount of feathers with the smallest possible amount of hissing.'

What makes good tax policy?

Not everyone, however, has seen tax policy as an exercise in cunning and cynicism. Adam Smith (Figure 15), in his major work *The Wealth of Nations* published in 1776, set out four principles, or 'canons' which should govern tax policy.

1   Equity of contributions: 'The subjects of every state ought to contribute towards the support of the government, as nearly as possible, in proportion to their respective abilities; that is, in proportion to the revenue which they respectively enjoy under the protection of the state.'

2 Certainty of tax liabilities: 'The tax which each individual is bound to pay ought to be certain, and not arbitrary. The time of payment, the manner of payment, the quantity to be paid, ought all to be clear and plain to the contributor, and to every other person. Where it is otherwise, every person subject to the tax is put more or less in the power of the tax-gatherer, who can either aggravate the tax...or extort...some present or perquisite to himself.'

3 Convenience of payment: 'Every tax ought to be levied at the time, or in the manner, in which it is most likely to be convenient for the contributor to pay it.'

4 Minimization of costs: 'Every tax ought to...take out and to keep out of the pockets of the people as little as possible over and above what it brings into the public treasury of the state,...in the four following ways. First, the levying of it may require a great number of officers, whose salaries may eat up the greater part of the produce of the tax...Secondly, it may obstruct the industry of the people, and...may thus diminish, or perhaps destroy, some of the funds which might enable them more easily to [pay]. Thirdly, by the forfeitures and other penalties which those unfortunate individuals incur who attempt unsuccessfully to evade the tax, it may frequently ruin them, and thereby put an end to the benefit which the community might have received from the employment of their capitals...Fourthly, by subjecting the people to the frequent visits and the odious examination of the tax-gatherers, it may expose them to much unnecessary trouble, vexation, and oppression...It is in some one or other of these four different ways that taxes are frequently so much more burdensome to the people than they are beneficial to the sovereign.'

Adam Smith's canons of taxation are surprisingly consistent with the way in which modern economic analysis approaches tax policy. The first and fourth canons, in particular, foreshadow the more modern concepts of 'equity' and 'efficiency', which sit at the heart of modern economic theorizing. Smith's second and third canons

15. The economist Adam Smith (1723–98).

address issues no less important, but ones which probably play
more of a role in the thinking of practical administrators than of
economists—the importance of ensuring that taxation is based on
clear rules, so as to leave little scope for arbitrary abuse of power
in the tax system, and the practical importance of having taxes
collected in a convenient manner.

Smith's discussion of the fourth canon sketches out four important aspects of the costs of taxation: the operating costs of the revenue authorities, the economic costs imposed by taxation through its impact on behaviour, the costs of activities which are required to prevent tax evasion, and the 'compliance costs' borne by taxpayers themselves in their contact with the tax system.

Where Smith's canons differ from contemporary economics is in their lack of clear guidance about how to balance the various considerations, and in particular what to do when the canons conflict in their recommendations.

As we have seen in earlier chapters, the perspective of modern economic analysis sees tax policy typically in terms of 'efficiency' and 'equity' objectives (where 'efficiency' encompasses the aim of minimizing the distortionary effects of taxation discussed in Chapter 4). Frequently these two goals are in opposition: for example, a higher marginal rate of tax on income (the additional tax paid when income increases) increases the distributional progressivity of the tax system, but it also increases labour market distortions.

The economics literature on 'optimal taxation', beginning with the work of James Mirrlees, considers the structure of taxes that will maximize a social welfare function, giving weight to both efficiency and equity goals. This approach makes the trade-offs explicit, and makes it possible to see how far particular policy recommendations depend on the weighting being given to equity in the analysis.

Although the economics of taxation is important, and we neglect the economic costs of taxation at our peril, we need to recognize that taxation is first and foremost a political issue. Tax policy is often a major election issue, and short-term political objectives may conflict with long-term rationality. Governments face pressures both from voters and from business lobbyists, and have to balance these pressures and interests in developing their tax policy. The tax system cannot be designed as a purely technocratic issue, and implemented as the outcome of a sophisticated backroom calculation. Ultimately it is the political process that decides on taxes and tax reform.

'Neutrality' as a guiding principle for tax policy

If the tax system is not to experience a chaotic sequence of random changes, some of them promoted by self-interested lobbies and others dreamed up by creative politicians, it is crucial that tax policy-making should be governed by clearly articulated principles, ideally commanding a degree of consent across the political spectrum. These principles need to be able to accommodate the shifts in priority that may come from changes in political control without the need for destabilizing waves of change in the fundamentals of the tax system.

No such principles fully conform to what economists might recommend as the optimal tax treatment of each particular activity. This almost certainly would turn on features of economic behaviour—elasticities and other behavioural responses to taxation—that can be measured only with great difficulty, and in some cases with little precision and confidence.

However, the notion of 'neutrality' as a guiding principle for tax policy has much to commend it. In essence it is a maxim that tax revenues should be raised with the least possible disturbance to economic activity—and as such it is broadly consistent with the concept of economic efficiency in taxation. It is, of course, impossible to raise significant revenues without affecting economic behaviour. The notion of neutrality suggests, however, a way of keeping this effect to a necessary minimum, in particular by ensuring that similar—and closely substitutable—activities are not subject to unjustified differences in tax treatment.

The value of neutrality as a principle is not only—or even primarily—its economic merits. As John Kay has argued, one great advantage of a rule that taxes should be neutral in their treatment of different activities is that it constrains the scope for sectoral lobbying. 'Not to have such a presumption', he writes, 'requires us to listen to the oil company, the mortgage lenders, the life assurance companies.' The government could find itself with little defence against well-resourced special pleading by companies and industries anxious to reduce the taxes they pay.

Where does the principle of neutrality in taxation then lead us in terms of practical policy? Its main implication is that similar activities should face the same taxation. Different forms of saving should be taxed equally; different industries should face the same taxes and should not be accorded special privileges and favourable treatment; different forms of corporate organization and financing should be taxed on an equivalent basis—a complex issue, well beyond the scope of this small book—and similar goods and services should all be taxed at the same rate.

Internationally, it implies that tax structures should not confer national preference or protection, and that national differences in revenue systems should not be manipulated for competitive advantage.

Beyond these general policy maxims, however, tax policies based on neutrality in the taxation of similar activities would offer extensive scope for different policy judgements about the scale of the public sector, the overall burden of taxation, and its distribution across the population. As a principle to guide tax policy, neutrality can still accommodate substantial differences in political choice and policy judgement, especially with respect to the priority to be given to equity and income redistribution. While changes in the political wind may of course lead to changes in taxation, the principle of neutrality may have scope to accommodate some of the more fundamental changes in political principle without excessive disturbance to the organization of the tax system.

In the following three sections we look at three key policy issues that lie at the heart of current tax policy controversy in many countries: the scope for radical simplification of the tax system, the case for a single-rate income tax, and the case for exempting basic goods such as food from sales taxes. We then look at an area of policy where departures from neutrality have strong justification as a way to correct failures and distortions that would otherwise arise in economic activity—the use of taxes in environmental policy. We conclude by looking at the future of tax policy: How are the ideas and principles discussed in this book likely to be affected by the increasing globalization of the world economy and by technological change?

Tax simplification

Proposals for radical income tax simplification are a seductive idea, with considerable political resonance in many countries. Existing tax legislation in nearly all countries is hugely complex—typically many hundreds of pages. Taxpayers struggle to comprehend the system, and often have to fill in long, complex tax returns which they barely understand. How much taxpayer time could be saved if the tax return was reduced to a handful of questions that would fit on the back of a postcard!

Considerable simplification would be achieved in many countries by eliminating the myriad allowances and deductions which can be set against taxpayers' income tax. The income tax system in the United States, for example, allows taxpayers to offset many deductions against their taxable income, including pension scheme contributions, mortgage interest, state and local taxes, charitable contributions, college tuition fees, house-moving costs, and business expenses.

Many of these have their origins in political and economic pressures in the distant past, but all add to the complexity of taxation, and can create unnecessary loopholes which weaken the revenue-raising effectiveness of the system. Taken together, the effect of these allowances and deductions is to narrow quite sharply the tax base—the income on which tax is charged—with the effect that higher rates have to be charged to raise a given revenue than if the income tax system had applied to a wider definition of income.

In countries such as the United States where there are extensive deductions and allowances that reduce taxpayers' taxable income, there is the opportunity for a 'base-broadening' tax reform that raises the same total tax revenue while reducing tax rates. Eliminating deductions and other special provisions would broaden the tax base sufficiently to allow a much lower tax rate to be set, whilst maintaining tax revenue. The same revenue could be collected—and taxpayers would, on average, pay the same amount in tax—but this could be achieved with lower tax rates and with less economic distortion.

Not all countries have a tax system with a large number of allowances, deductions, and special tax privileges for particular activities or groups. The UK income tax, for example, is relatively straightforward, with relatively few deductions which can be set against taxable income. Consequently there is relatively little scope for a base-broadening reform that would permit reductions in UK income tax rates.

But how realistic is tax simplification? Much tax complexity arises from efforts to prevent the exploitation of tax loopholes. For example, many countries have extremely complex legislation to tax capital gains. The reason for this is not because they expect to collect large revenues from capital gains taxes, but because the capital gains legislation protects income tax revenues by discouraging taxpayers from turning income into capital gains.

More generally, many tax loopholes arise because of differences in the fiscal treatment of income paid in different ways. Many countries—including the UK—tax wages and other 'earned' income at a different rate from bank interest, share dividends, and other 'unearned' income. Mostly, earnings are taxed more heavily, if only because they tend to be subject to social contributions as well as the main income tax. The effect of this is to create a strong incentive for employers to try to pay as much as possible of their employees' remuneration in forms that would count as unearned rather than earned income, and a lot of effort is put into devising ingenious avoidance schemes that achieve this. The scope for avoidance—and the need, then, for complicated anti-avoidance principles in legislation—is greatly diminished, if tax systems do not seek to make distinctions between different categories of activity that are potentially substitutable, and which have blurred or ambiguous boundaries. This is easier said than done, of course, but if tax simplification is not to open the door to widespread avoidance, it places serious constraints on the philosophy and structure of the tax system.

There would be substantial administrative advantages in moving towards a simpler, more uniform tax system, with greater uniformity in the tax treatment of different income sources, but this seems hard to achieve, and, perhaps, even harder to maintain.

A flat-rate income tax?

A different issue—though one that is frequently conflated with proposals for simplifying the tax base—is the case for reducing the higher rates of income tax charged on high-income earners, and, even more radically, for levying income tax at the same rate at all levels of income.

Some argue that the disincentive effects of the highest tax rates are so large that reducing tax rates would actually increase tax revenues. The so-called 'Laffer curve' reflects this possibility: when existing taxes are very high, a cut in tax rates may actually increase revenues by stimulating so much growth in the tax base that this more than compensates for the reduced rate of tax that is being charged.

One important way in which this might happen is by encouraging internationally mobile taxpayers to return, or not to relocate their activities abroad. Also, cutting tax rates could improve incentives for labour supply, as discussed in Chapter 4. Both these effects expand the domestic tax base, and if they are sufficiently strong, the revenue-increasing effect of the larger tax base could outweigh the revenue-reducing effect of the lower rate of tax. Identifying the logical possibility that this could happen is, however, a far cry from demonstrating that tax cuts actually increase revenues in practice; this will depend on the level of existing taxation and the magnitude in practice of the behavioural responses to taxation.

Flat-rate income taxes have been introduced in many of the formerly centrally planned economies of eastern Europe and the former USSR. Often this seems to have been a dramatic statement of intent by governments committed to introducing more market-orientated economic policies. There could be few clearer ways of signalling that economic policy was no longer to be governed by Marx's principle 'from each according to his abilities; to each according to his needs' than eliminating higher tax rates on the rich.

The first flat-rate income tax reforms in the former communist countries were in the Baltic states. In 1994 Estonia introduced a flat-rate income tax of 26 per cent to replace the rates of 16–33 per cent previously charged. Lithuania set a uniform tax rate of 33 per cent—in fact its highest pre-reform tax rate—and Latvia set a uniform rate of 25 per cent.

The flat-rate income tax reform that really captured the imagination of policy-makers was, however, the Russian reform of

2001. Unlike the Baltic states, which had set their uniform income tax at relatively high rates, Russia's flat-rate tax was at a low rate—13 per cent—barely higher than its lowest pre-reform income tax rate. Tax rates for higher income earners were cut dramatically. Despite the sharp reduction in the average rate of income tax, however, income tax revenues were remarkably buoyant. In the year after the reform, revenues increased by 46 per cent, a rise of some 26 per cent after allowing for the effects of inflation. This seemed like dramatic confirmation of the strength of the Laffer curve effect.

However, much to the chagrin of radical reformers and low-tax campaigners, the story of Russia's revenue-increasing tax cuts fell apart under detailed scrutiny by International Monetary Fund (IMF) economists. They noted that the rise in revenue seemed to have little connection with the change in tax rates. The majority of taxpayers were largely unaffected by the reforms, paying much the same tax rate after the reform as before, while a small proportion of taxpayers benefited from very large cuts in income tax rates. If the flat-rate tax had really been responsible for the sharp growth in tax revenues, it would be reasonable to expect this to have come from the taxpayers who had been affected by the reforms. The opposite, however, seems to have been the case: the strongest growth in income tax payments came from those who were untouched by the change in tax rates, and there was a dramatic fall in the proportion of revenue contributed by the high-income taxpayers who benefited from the reform. Other factors than cuts in tax rates seem to explain the overall rise in tax revenues, in particular the much more muscular approach to tax enforcement that had been introduced by the newly elected President Putin. The IMF economists concluded with a warning of the risks of over-enthusiastic supply-side reforms: 'Tax-cutting reforms of this kind should not be expected to pay for themselves by greater work effort or improved compliance.'

Flat-rate income tax reforms may, nonetheless, have played an important role in simplifying tax administration in the challenging environment of the post-Soviet economies, where the tax authorities struggled to come to terms with the rapidly developing private sector, without the information base and legal resources needed to ensure compliance, and where economic policy-makers wanted to assert a sharp break with previous views of the role of the state in economic activity. Is there, however, any mileage in similar reforms, based on a single flat rate of income tax, outside eastern Europe and the former USSR?

There is little doubt that a single rate of income tax has some practical advantages. Many of the arrangements for deduction of tax at source, on bank interest and share dividends for example, can be greatly simplified without the need for subsequent adjustment to reflect the precise tax rate applicable to each individual taxpayer. Fewer tax 'boundaries' would need to be policed if different taxpayers all faced the same rate of tax.

A reduction in the tax rate on high earners might also improve tax compliance—in other words, reducing the use of schemes for tax evasion and avoidance—if the main deterrent for taxpayers using these schemes is in practice the cost rather than the risks involved. Taxpayers may then be more inclined to comply, and the tax base would be increased (though there is no evidence that this effect would, in itself, be strong enough to pay for the reform).

The most obvious objection to a single rate of income tax would appear to be its distributional effects. Reducing tax rates on higher incomes while maintaining constant overall revenues would seem to require an increase in the tax burden on lower incomes and greater inequality. In fact, the distributional effects of some of the reforms actually implemented have been less clear-cut. Many reforms, such the flat tax in Estonia for example, combined a uniform tax rate with a higher initial tax-free allowance. Although the tax rate faced by low earners increased, their overall tax bill was reduced by the higher tax-free allowance. In terms of the distributional effects, the losers from this reform were in the middle of the income scale, with gains being made by low- and high-income-earners.

Figure 16 illustrates the trade-off between a low flat tax rate and distributional equity using results from a simulation by Clemens Fuest, Andreas Peichl, and Thilo Schaefer of a hypothetical flat tax reform in Germany. The two simulated scenarios both raise the same revenue as the existing income tax system in 2007, which had marginal tax rates ranging between 15 per cent and 45 per cent. The first scenario maintains the existing tax-free allowance, and sets the flat-rate tax at 27 per cent. Households at the very bottom of the income scale are largely unaffected, because they pay virtually no tax in any case. Most income taxpayers would pay more under the flat tax, in some cases substantially more, but large gains would be made by the richest taxpayers, those in the top income decile, whose annual tax bill would fall on average by more than €3,000. The second scenario addresses the adverse effect on income inequality by increasing the annual tax-free allowance by about one-third, but in order to maintain revenues must then set the flat-rate income tax at a much higher rate of 32 per cent. The effect of the higher allowance is to reduce the additional tax payments by middle-income households, and the higher rate of tax reduces the gains made by the rich. The study also shows that, with the lower tax rates in the first scenario, there is a modest reduction in the distortionary cost of income taxation, and a small increase in employment (of about 0.3 per cent), but with the higher tax rate needed in the second scenario these labour market benefits are wiped out. The trade-off between equity and efficiency in these reforms is very stark indeed.

Such a pattern of gainers and losers makes the politics of a flat tax reform rather unpromising. The conventional 'median voter' wisdom about self-interested voting on economic issues would

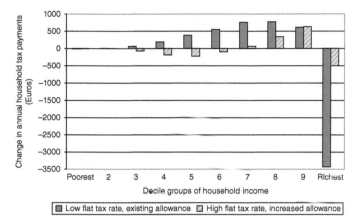

16. Who gains and who loses from a flat-rate income tax? Changes in household income tax payments under a simulated flat-rate income tax for Germany (Study by Fuest, Peichl, and Schaefer, 2008).

place the swing voter somewhere in the middle of the income range, with political parties offering policies which converge on the interests of this group of the electorate. A reform that does harm to the interests of this group, while benefiting the rich, would seem to run directly counter to the way in which modern political competition seems to operate.

Of course, it might be possible to implement a flat-rate income tax with the support of those in the middle of the income distribution, and, at the same time, to provide adequate protection for the interests of the poor, if it is implemented as part of a wider package of measures. But if revenue is not to be lost in the course of the reform, the income tax component of the package will need to have relatively high marginal tax rates. And almost all conceivable reform packages based on flat-rate income tax share one very clear characteristic: the most substantial gain would accrue to the richest taxpayers.

Sales taxes and the poor

Could simplification through greater uniformity in taxation also be applied to sales taxes? Many countries with sales taxes such as VAT levy the tax at various different tax rates. Member states of the European Union are permitted to levy reduced rates of VAT on food and certain other 'distributionally sensitive' goods and services. Most choose to do so: only Denmark levies VAT at the same rate for all taxable goods and services. The UK takes matters to the extreme of 'zero-rating' food, water, children's clothing, public transport, books and newspapers, and some other items, and applies a low rate of VAT—5 per cent—to household supplies of electricity and gas.

Outside the EU, VAT systems often have a rather less complicated structure of tax rates. Many of the developing countries which have adopted VAT in recent years have chosen to apply it at a single uniform rate, though some have followed the EU in charging lower tax rates on goods and services which typically form a large part of the spending of poorer households.

In practical terms there are huge advantages in operating a sales tax system like VAT at a single rate. The amount of information which the tax authorities need to collect and verify is much more limited than when sales are taxed at various different rates. In a single-rate system, all the authorities need to know is the total level of sales of each business, not a detailed breakdown of sales between product categories. The information which firms need to collect and supply to the tax authorities is correspondingly reduced.

Where different goods are taxed at different rates, taxpayers and the revenue authorities can find themselves embroiled in time-consuming, costly, and—often—surreal litigation over the correct tax classification of particular transactions. To avoid erosion of VAT revenues the UK revenue authorities have been forced to defend the tax treatment of various food items: well-paid lawyers have spent days in court debating whether 'Jaffa cakes', a chocolate-coated biscuit-sized product, should count as a (zero-rated) cake or a (standard-rated) biscuit for VAT purposes, and whether freshly squeezed orange juice should count as (zero-rated) fruit or a (standard-rated) soft drink. In each case, what was at stake was tax revenue equal to 17.5 per cent of the total value of sales of the product: a huge windfall to an individual firm which succeeds in challenging the tax classification of their product. To individual firms, it is well worth spending significant sums of money on litigation of this sort, if there is a chance of shifting some of their products into the lower rate category, but to the revenue authorities the ambiguity over the definition of product categories is a wasteful diversion of time and resources that could be better spent elsewhere.

In any case, differentiating sales tax rates makes a feeble contribution to helping the poor. The problem is that, while the poor may spend a higher proportion of their income on 'necessities' such as food, and a lower proportion of their income on less-essential goods and luxuries, the rich spend more on pretty much everything. As a result, whatever benefit is given to poorer households by charging a low VAT rate on food, the benefit this gives to richer households is greater, since they spend more money on food like nearly everything else.

We can think of the VAT revenue forgone by charging a low rate of VAT on food as a form of subsidy, paid to households in proportion to their purchases of food. The subsidy through low VAT on food is larger relative to income for poorer households, but it is a smaller amount of cash than the rich receive.

Figures from the 2007 OECD Economic Survey of Mexico illustrate this clearly (Figure 17). The VAT system in Mexico zero-rates food and some other goods and services, reflecting concern about the impact of taxing food on the living standards of

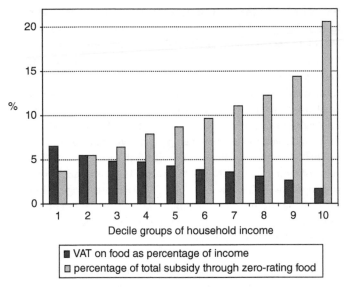

17. Who gets the benefit if VAT is not levied on food? Distribution of household payments of VAT on food and the implicit subsidy from zero-rating food across household income groups in Mexico, 2005.

the poor. As the darker bars in the graph show, charging VAT on food would create a heavier burden on poorer households than on the better-off. For the poorest two deciles—the poorest 20 per cent of the population—the extra tax would amount to 6 per cent of income, compared with 2 per cent for the richest 20 per cent of the population. Eliminating the zero-rating of food would thus be relatively more harmful to the poor than to the rich.

On the other hand, it can be seen that the amount of help that is given to the poor by VAT zero-rating of food is only a small part of the VAT revenue forgone. The paler bars in the figure show the distribution of the benefit of VAT zero-rating across income groups in cash terms; in other words, the percentage of the total subsidy which goes to each income group. It is clear that the benefit of VAT zero-rating in money terms rises steadily up the income scale. For every $100 forgone in tax revenue through VAT zero-rating in Mexico, more than $40 goes to the top 20 per cent of households, and less than $10 to the poorest 20 per cent of households. Zero-rating food helps the poor, but it does so very wastefully: $100 must be spent in order to transfer less than $10 to the poorest 20 per cent of the population. In this case, Arthur Okun's bucket (see Chapter 4) is very leaky indeed.

The question, of course, is whether there would be a more effective way of using the same money. Could we target other forms of assistance to the poor more effectively than by VAT zero-rating of food? The answer is an unequivocal 'yes'. Even giving each household in the population an equal lump-sum amount from the proceeds of VAT on food would help the poor more than zero-rating would do. Still more sophisticated packages can be devised that achieve effective compensation of the poor for the effects of VAT on food at even lower cost, for example by devoting part of the additional revenues to increasing the value of means-tested social benefits paid to poorer households.

None of this analysis would come as a surprise to tax policy-makers in the UK Treasury or other finance ministries. It is widely recognized that the largest beneficiaries of reduced VAT rates are the better-off, and that only a fraction of the additional tax resources generated by taxing food at the standard rate would be required to provide help more effectively to poorer households. Nevertheless, reduced VAT rates on food and other necessities have proved remarkably durable, and few countries have dared to propose abolishing them. Why might this be so?

One possibility is that governments are scared of a backlash from better-off voters who dislike being asked to pay more. Another reason, no doubt, is that it may be harder to explain that there are better ways of helping the poor than it is to make the point that the extra VAT would be a large part of poorer households' budgets. A further, intriguing, possibility is that what underpins public resistance to imposing VAT on food is not just driven by its effectiveness in helping the poor, but by a wider view that there are some things, such as food, that, in principle, simply should not be taxed. This may well be a principle which would command wide support, but what is clear from the data above is that this view comes at a considerable price.

Taxation and the environment

In recent years environmental policy-makers have become increasingly aware of the costs and limitations of conventional 'command-and-control' environmental regulation, in which a public regulatory agency sets legal limits on a firm's polluting emissions, or requires it to use particular technologies or equipment for pollution control. They recognize that this approach to environmental regulation can be too rigid and excessively costly for the regulated firms and the economy as a whole. Given more flexibility, firms might be able to find cheaper ways of reducing emissions that would achieve the same environmental benefits at lower cost.

Environmental policy-makers have increasingly turned to more flexible 'economic instruments' as a way of reducing the costs of environmental regulation. A tax on polluting emissions—say, a tax per kilogram of nitrogen oxides emitted by power stations and large industrial boilers and furnaces—would give firms an incentive to reduce emissions whenever the cost of emissions reductions was less than the tax. It would ensure that emission reductions were concentrated on those that could be achieved at low cost, and polluters for whom the costs of abatement were excessively high would have the option of paying the tax instead. A system of tradable pollution permits achieves a similar outcome. It sets a limit on overall pollution by limiting the number of permits issued, and trading will then ensure that permits end up in the hands of the firms with the highest abatement costs. Moreover, both emissions taxes and tradable permits provide an ongoing incentive for further innovation in pollution control technologies, since firms face a price for any pollution they still emit. By contrast, under conventional regulation, a firm that has met its legal requirements faces no incentive to cut its emissions further.

There have been some very successful applications of both emissions trading and environmental taxes in the past two decades. The US Acid Rain Program, for example, used emissions trading between power stations to facilitate a much more rapid reduction in their sulphur dioxide emissions than would have been possible with more conventional approaches to emissions regulation. A number of countries have used taxes on product packaging and waste disposal to achieve reductions in unnecessary packaging and to stimulate greater recycling. And taxes on motor fuels and vehicles have been restructured to encourage a shift to less-polluting fuels (unleaded petrol, low-sulphur diesel, etc.), and to incentivize the development of more fuel-efficient vehicles.

How much scope is there for tax policy to go further in this direction? There are two areas in particular where taxes and emissions trading could be used to strengthen incentives for environmental improvement. Higher taxes on fossil-fuel energy are needed to stimulate the wide-ranging changes in household and industrial behaviour that will be needed if global greenhouse gas emissions are to be reduced and the risk of catastrophic climate change averted. Systematic taxation of traffic congestion—'congestion charging'—offers the prospect of tackling the otherwise intractable problems of urban traffic congestion. Both could potentially raise quite significant revenues, although introducing congestion charging would weaken the case for retaining the present very high level of motor fuel taxes in many European countries.

Tax policy: the future

At the start of this book we saw the massive expansion in tax revenues over the past fifty years. Over the OECD area as a whole, tax revenues increased more than fourfold in real terms, as economic growth led to higher revenues, and more tax was raised through higher social contributions and the introduction of VAT. At the same time, the revenues from taxes on international trade fell as the result of successive rounds of trade liberalization. What changes might we expect to see in the coming decades?

The most powerful force shaping future tax policy is likely to be the increasing globalization of economic activity, which means that countries' economies will be closely inter-connected, and their economic policies—including tax policies—increasingly constrained by the pressures of international economic competition. Policy choices in other countries will severely limit the margin for manoeuvre in domestic tax policy.

Globalization has made tax bases more mobile. Capital and investment, the production of goods and services, and, indeed, employment can move much more freely between countries, and decisions about where to invest and produce are likely to be increasingly influenced by taxation. The effect of this increased mobility is that countries will lose—and indeed have already lost—substantial de facto fiscal sovereignty. Countries that try to set tax rates for capital or other highly mobile tax bases that are higher than the tax rates elsewhere will find that they lose tax base to their competitors as mobile activities move abroad. In markets such as capital markets with a high level of international integration, countries may have negligible power to set tax rates that differ from the rates ruling elsewhere; if they were to do so they would suffer a substantial capital outflow, which would continue until the net-of-tax return available to the investor was equalized with the net-of-tax return available in other locations. It is this process that is already thought to have shifted much of the burden of corporate taxes in smaller economies away from capital and onto less mobile tax bases such as unskilled labour.

Countries that try to have a tax system that is more redistributive than elsewhere may find that the losers from this redistribution move elsewhere, leaving only those who might have expected to gain. Some pessimists see in this process the end of redistributive public policy altogether, and the end of the welfare state. Even if this exaggerates the severity of the constraint that international competition places on redistributive policies, the reality is that countries' fiscal choices will be increasingly constrained by competitive pressures. Highly redistributive policies will carry a significant cost in the form of outflows of highly skilled labour and capital, which will increase the cost of redistribution.

The pressures on tax policy from the effects of greater mobility of commodities, firms, and people in the globalized economy will be exacerbated by the impact of the internet, which is already reshaping certain areas of the economy, and which creates new difficulties for tax systems which are, in the main, designed to deal with transactions in physical goods. Internet-based retailers have proved adept at exploiting opportunities to have their products taxed in countries offering them the most favourable tax regime, both for the taxes they must charge on sales, and the corporate taxes levied on their profits. Some of the opportunities that internet-based companies have been able to exploit to reduce the taxes charged on their sales and profits are loopholes that have been exposed in legislation which was not drafted with the internet in mind, and, over time, many of these loopholes are likely to be closed. However, while the internet may not—as some have feared—spell complete catastrophe for the tax system, it has undoubtedly amplified the impact of globalization on the fiscal system by reducing the costs of mobility and expanding the range of activities that can be shifted to locations offering a more favourable tax treatment.

Unlike economic competition between firms, which tends to promote efficiency and lower prices to consumers, fiscal competition between countries is not a benign process. Tax havens, in particular, exploit their ability to offer a lower tax regime which undercuts the rates of tax elsewhere; they are not offering any greater efficiency or any other positive advantage, but only the opportunity to sidestep taxes levied elsewhere. Countries which compete to grab tax base from other countries impose a costly burden on other countries, raising their cost of revenue-raising and limiting the range of tax policy choices that countries can make.

A further aspect of globalization is the growing significance and power of large-scale multinational enterprises operating on a transnational basis. Multinationals have the opportunity to shift a significant proportion of their profits into countries where they will be taxed less heavily by manipulating the internal charges—the 'transfer prices'—at which they book trades between their subsidiaries located in different countries. Profits can be shifted out of a country where they would be taxed heavily by raising the price which that subsidiary must pay other parts of the group for supplies or the use of intellectual property, such as patents or brand rights, and by under-charging for its own sales within the group. The 'arm's length' principle espoused by the OECD is intended to constrain this, by forcing firms to set their internal charging on a basis that mirrors the prices that would be charged for an equivalent transaction between wholly independent firms. But it is often very difficult to implement this principle, since there may be no directly equivalent arm's length transactions to use as a benchmark. This is a particular problem with multinationals which earn a substantial proportion of their profits from a brand image or other special advantage that they possess. Such firms have a considerable degree of latitude in shifting profits to lower tax countries and tax havens. At the very least, the grey area around transfer pricing offers considerable scope for firms to challenge the tax assessments they receive, and the tax authorities must then decide whether to spend resources on a legal battle to preserve their revenues.

One way of restoring some measure of tax sovereignty is, paradoxically, through international coordination and harmonization. If countries collectively agree ground-rules that limit the scope for tax competition that could drive tax rates downwards, all may benefit by being able to raise revenues without the erosion of those tax bases most affected by mobility. There is nothing equitable about a tax system in which the mobile—and perhaps predominantly rich—can avoid taxation, while the burden of taxation ends up borne by those unable to escape. Nor is there anything efficient about allowing unrestricted international tax competition to erode parts of the tax base. A continuing feature of tax policy over the coming years is likely to be a difficult and protracted international debate over whether countries are willing to reach some form of agreement to limit the scope for tax competition and the operation of international tax havens.

Glossary

Average rate of tax. The total tax paid, as a percentage of the tax base. So, for an income tax, the taxpayer's total income tax payment, expressed as a percentage of their taxable income.

Compliance cost. The cost incurred by the taxpayer in their interactions with the tax authorities, including the time and other costs incurred in completing a tax return and making tax payments.

Corporate income tax, *see* **Corporation tax**.

Corporation tax. A tax on the profits of incorporated businesses.

Distortionary effects. Changes in the behaviour of individual or business taxpayers induced by the presence of taxation. For example, increasing the rate of tax on some item may lead people to buy less of it, switching to alternatives they would not have chosen in the absence of tax.

Efficiency. In the economics of taxation, efficiency means raising revenue at least economic cost, i.e. with the minimum **excess burden**.

Excess burden. The total economic cost of raising a given revenue, over and above the value of the revenue itself. The excess burden includes the economic value of the distortionary effects of taxes; in other words, the reduction in taxpayers' living standards arising from tax-induced changes in behaviour.

Excise duty/tax. A sales tax levied on certain commodities such as alcoholic drinks, tobacco products, or motor fuels.

Flat-rate income tax. Tax levied at a uniform percentage rate on all taxpayers.

Incidence. Where the burden of taxation is borne.

Lump-sum tax. Taxation taking the form of a fixed amount for each taxpayer, irrespective of any characteristics or behaviour under their control.

Marginal rate of tax. The additional tax paid as a result of a small increase in the tax base. So, for an income tax, the marginal tax rate is the additional income tax paid on an additional pound or dollar of income.

Payroll tax. A tax levied on the total wage bill of a company.

Poll tax. A tax taking the form of an equal amount per taxpayer.

Progressive taxation. A pattern of taxation across households in which the poor pay a *lower percentage* of income in tax than the rich.

Regressive taxation. A pattern of taxation across households in which the poor pay a *higher percentage* of income in tax than the rich.

Retail sales tax. A tax on the aggregate value of retail sales by a business (i.e. a tax on sales made to individual consumers).

Social contributions. Taxes, typically levied on income or payroll, which are specifically allocated to fund social insurance benefits such as unemployment and sickness insurance, public pensions, or health care.

Tax avoidance. Actions taken by a taxpayer to reduce the amount of tax they pay through legal means; this can include the use of contrived or artificial devices.

Tax base. The amount or quantity on which taxation is levied.

Tax compliance. Ensuring payment of all tax properly due, without tax evasion.

Tax evasion. Failing to pay some of the tax that would be due—generally, either by concealing or by under-reporting income or other taxable transactions.

Transfer pricing. The price charged for transactions between branches of the same multinational enterprise. By choosing a higher or lower transfer price an enterprise could shift profits between subsidiaries located in different countries, to ensure that they accrue in a country where they will be taxed less.

Turnover tax. A tax on the aggregate value of sales by a business, including sales both to individual consumers and to other businesses.

Value-added tax (VAT). A tax on the value of sales by a business, in which the business can offset the amount of tax paid on its purchases of goods and services against the tax due on its sales.

Further reading

General recommendations

Institute for Fiscal Studies, *Tax by Design: The Mirrlees Review* (OUP, 2011).

Paul Johnson, 'Tax without design: recent developments in UK Tax Policy', *Fiscal Studies*, 35 (2014): 243–73.

JA Kay and MA King, *The British Tax System* (OUP, 1978).

Bernard Salanié, *The Economics of Taxation* (MIT Press, 2003).

Chapter 3: Who bears the tax burden?

Wiji Arulampalam, Michael P Devereux, and Giorgia Maffini, 'The direct incidence of corporate income tax on wages', *European Economic Review*, 56 (2012): 1038–54.

Alan J Auerbach, 'Who bears the corporate tax? A review of what we know', *Tax Policy and the Economy*, 20 (2006): 1–40.

Timothy J Besley and Harvey S Rosen, 'Sales tax and prices: an empirical analysis', *National Tax Journal*, 52 (1999): 157–78.

Jonathan Gruber, 'The incidence of payroll taxation: evidence from Chile', *Journal of Labor Economics*, 15 (1997): 72–101.

Chapter 4: Taxation and the economy

Christopher Heady, 'Optimal taxation as a guide to tax policy', in Michael P Devereux (ed), *The Economics of Tax Policy* (OUP, 1996).

Costas Meghir and David Phillips, 'Labour supply and taxes', in J Mirrlees, S Adam, T Besley, R Blundell, S Bond, R Chote,

M Gammie, P Johnson, G Myles, and J Poterba (eds), *Dimensions of Tax Design: The Mirrlees Review* (OUP, 2010).

OECD (Organisation for Economic Co-operation and Development), *Taxation and Employment*, OECD Tax Policy Studies No. 21 (OECD, 2011).

Joel Slemrod and Jon Bakija, *Taxing Ourselves: A Citizen's Guide to the Great Debate Over Tax Reform* (MIT Press, 1996).

Chapter 5: Tax evasion and enforcement

James Andreoni, Brian Erard, and Jonathan Feinstein, 'Tax compliance', *Journal of Economic Literature*, XXXVI (1998): 818–60.

Frank Cowell, *Cheating the Government: The Economics of Evasion* (MIT Press, 1990).

Michael Keen and Stephen Smith, 'VAT fraud and evasion: what do we know and what can be done?', *National Tax Journal*, 59 (2006): 861–87.

Henrik J Kleven, Martin B Knudsen, Claus T Kreiner, Søren Pedersen, and Emmanuel Saez, 'Unwilling or unable to cheat? Evidence from a randomised tax audit experiment in Denmark', NBER Working Paper No. 15769 (2010).

Mike O'Doherty, 'Thinking and learning in the tax evasion game', *Fiscal Studies*, 35 (2014): 297–339.

Joel Slemrod, 'Cheating ourselves: the economics of tax evasion', *Journal of Economic Perspectives*, 21 (2007): 25–48.

Michael Wenzel, 'Misperceptions of social norms about tax compliance: from theory to intervention', *Journal of Economic Psychology*, 26 (2005): 862–83.

Chapter 6: Issues in tax policy

Stuart Adam and James Browne, *Options for a UK 'Flat Tax'—Some Simple Simulations* (Institute for Fiscal Studies, August 2006).

Peter Diamond and Emmanuel Saez, 'The case for a progressive tax: from basic research to policy recommendations', *Journal of Economic Perspectives*, 25 (2011): 165–90.

Clemens Fuest, Andreas Peichl, and Thilo Schaefer, 'Is a flat tax feasible in a grown-up democracy of Western Europe? A simulation study for Germany', *International Tax and Public Finance*, 15 (2008): 620–36.

Anna Ivanova, Alexander Klemm, and Michael Keen, 'The Russian flat tax reform', *Economic Policy*, 43 (2005): 397–444.

JA Kay, 'The social and political context of taxation', in Donal de Butleir and Frances Ruane (eds), *Governance and Policy In Ireland: Essays in Honour of Miriam Hederman O'Brien* (Institute of Public Administration, Dublin, 2003).

Michael Keen, Yitae Kim, and Ricardo Varsano, 'The flat tax(es): principles and evidence', *International Tax and Public Finance*, 15 (2008): 712–51.

OECD (Organisation for Economic Co-operation and Development), *Choosing a Broad Base—Low Rate Approach to Taxation*, OECD Tax Policy Studies No. 19 (OECD, 2010).

OECD (Organisation for Economic Co-operation and Development), *Fundamental Reform of Personal Income Tax*, OECD Tax Policy Studies No. 13 (OECD, 2006).

Further reading

Index

A

administrative costs of taxation 33, 49, 57, 99, 101, 106
alcoholic drinks, taxation of 14, 24–5
allowance, tax 18–19, 67–8, 73, 109–11
average rate of tax 19, 65, 73, 108, 123
avoidance 26, 81–3, 93, 105–6, 109, 123

B

benefits *see* social benefits
business rates (United Kingdom) 26, 44–5
business taxation 16, 25–7, 44
business-to-business (B2B) transactions 22, 23

C

capital gains tax 44, 105
capitalization effects 38, 61–2
carbon tax 29
cigarettes, taxation of 14, 21, 24–5
Colbert, Jean-Baptiste 98

collection (tax collection) 6–7, 25, 49, 95, 99–100
commodity taxation 33, 53–7, 103
community charge *see* poll tax
complexity, of taxation 104–6
compliance 75–96, 108–9, 123
compliance costs 49–50, 101, 123
consumption taxes 53–7, 72–4
coordination, international 121
corporation tax 13–14, 25–6, 50, 81–3, 90, 92, 123
corporate income tax *see* corporation tax
council tax (United Kingdom) 28, 46
cross-border shopping 25

D

deduction at source *see* withholding
deductions 18, 77–8, 104–5
Denmark 23, 91, 112
developing countries 21, 24, 27, 30, 112
distortionary effects of taxation 50–8, 60–2, 66–8, 72–3, 101, 104–5, 110, 123
distributional effects 40–7, 58–60, 66–7, 73, 101, 109–16

E

economic effects of taxation 48–74
efficiency, economic 51–6, 66–8, 99, 101–2, 123
employment, effects of taxation 37, 62–74, 110, 118
enforcement 91, 93–6, 108
environmental taxes 27, 29, 116–17
equity 19, 40–7, 58–60, 66–8, 93, 98–9, 101, 103, 110
European Community 1, 21, 23, 25, 30, 112
evasion 24, 75–96, 101, 109, 124
  individual risks and gains 83–7
  non-economic influences 87–9
  opportunities 76–83
  penalties 83–6, 94–5
  policy 93–6
  public attitudes 87–9, 96
  revenue losses 89–93
excess burden 50–6, 58, 123
excise duty/tax 13–14, 24–5, 44–6, 73, 93, 123

F

fairness *see* equity
flat-rate tax 106–11, 123
France 8, 10, 15, 16, 20–1, 23, 28, 49, 52, 71

G

Gandhi, Mahatma 97
General Agreement on Tariffs and Trade (GATT) 30
George, Henry 60–1
Germany 71, 110–11
globalization 118–21
Gross Domestic Product (GDP) 1, 9–10, 14, 16, 49

H

Holmes, Oliver Wendell, Jr 75–6

I

import duties 27, 30, 118
incidence 31–40, 44, 68, 73, 123
income effect 64–5
income-in-kind 18
income tax; *see also* corporate income tax 2, 13–15, 16–21, 25, 29, 31, 40, 43–50, 57, 62–74, 77–8, 80–1, 90–3, 104–11
inheritance taxes 27–9, 44
Institute for Fiscal Studies (IFS) 44
International Monetary Fund (IMF) 108
international trade 27, 30, 118–19
investment income, taxation of 13, 17, 25, 79

L

labour market
  effect of income tax 37–9, 62–74, 106–11
  effect of sales tax 62, 64, 72–4
Laffer curve 106–8
land taxation 6–8, 14, 27–8, 38, 57–62
landfill tax 29
local government taxation 2, 23, 26–8, 44, 49, 97–8, 104
lobbying 1, 15, 61, 101–3
loopholes 82, 105–6, 119
lump-sum tax 68, 124

M

marginal rate of tax 19–20, 65, 67–70, 72–4, 101, 106–11, 124
married couples, taxation of 18
Mexico 113–15

Index

Mirrlees, James 101
Mirrlees Review 47
morality 43, 76, 83, 87–9, 96
motor fuels, taxation of 2, 14, 24–5, 29, 117
motor vehicles, taxation of 21, 29
municipal taxes *see* local government taxation

N

Napoleonic wars 17
National Insurance Contributions 20–1, 44–5
natural resource taxes 27, 29
neutrality 102–4
non-distortionary taxation 57–62, 68
North Sea Oil taxation 29
Norway 29

O

Okun, Arthur 67–8, 115
optimal taxation 56–7, 101–2

P

participation tax rate 71–2
payroll tax 13–14, 37–8, 40, 57, 63, 124
peasants' revolt 98
pension contributions 18, 104
pensions 17, 20
politics and taxation 1–2, 4, 10–12, 15, 20, 43, 58, 61, 68, 97, 101–5, 110–11, 115–16
poll tax 2, 6, 58–60, 68, 98, 124
progressivity 42–7, 67, 73–4, 101, 124
property income 17
property tax 6, 8, 13–14, 25–8, 32–3, 38, 98

R

Ramsey, Frank 56–7
regressivity 42–7, 112–16, 124
retail sales tax 22–4, 33, 124
Russia, flat-rate tax 107–9

S

sales tax 13–5, 20–5, 33–7, 53–7, 72–4, 80–1, 112–16
savings, taxation of 1, 17, 52, 103
self-employment 13, 18, 49, 79–80, 87, 89–90
shifting, of tax burden 32–40, 72
simplification 104–6, 108–9, 112
Smith, Adam 98–101
social benefits, interaction with taxes 46–7, 65–66, 70–2, 115
social contributions 13–15, 20–1, 50, 106, 124
social security benefits *see* social benefits
social security contributions *see* social contributions
spending, taxes on 1, 2, 5, 10, 21–5, 44–5, 57, 72–4, 92, 112–16
see also sales tax; Value-Added Tax
stamp duty 28, 32–3
substitution effect 64–5
supply and demand 33–7, 53–6, 61

T

tariffs 30
tax base 5, 12, 17, 19, 26, 40, 56, 105–7, 118–21, 124
tax payments
household 44–7, 110–11, 113–15
tax policy 15, 97–121
tax privileges 15, 103–5
tax revenue
composition 13–16, 24–7, 29–30
costs of 49–51, 101–2

growth 8–10, 14–15, 118
lost through evasion 81–93
need for 1, 3, 7–8, 11, 15, 98
per head 13–14
relative to GDP 1, 8–10, 14
and tax rates 106–8
tax structure 12–30
tax wedge on earnings 68–74
taxation
definition 4–5
differences between countries
15–16, 18, 23, 26, 30
historical development 2, 5–10,
13–15, 17, 21, 24, 30, 48, 97–8
Thatcher, Margaret 97
Tolstoy, Leo 12, 13
transfer pricing 26, 82, 120, 124
turnover tax 124

U

United Kingdom 15–21, 23,
25–6, 28–9, 32, 49, 97–8,
105–6

United States of America 15, 16, 21,
23, 30, 49, 97, 104–5, 117

V

value-added tax (VAT) 14–15, 21–4,
72–4, 80–1, 112–16, 124
VAT gap 92–3

W

wages, impact of taxes 32, 37,
40–1, 68–9
wealth tax 27–8
window tax 51–3
withholding 20, 25, 50, 76, 78, 86,
93–4, 109
World Trade Organisation
(WTO) 30

Z

zero-rating, of VAT 22, 73,
112–16

Index

Expand your collection of
VERY SHORT INTRODUCTIONS

1. Classics
2. Music
3. Buddhism
4. Literary Theory
5. Hinduism
6. Psychology
7. Islam
8. Politics
9. Theology
10. Archaeology
11. Judaism
12. Sociology
13. The Koran
14. The Bible
15. Social and Cultural Anthropology
16. History
17. Roman Britain
18. The Anglo-Saxon Age
19. Medieval Britain
20. The Tudors
21. Stuart Britain
22. Eighteenth-Century Britain
23. Nineteenth-Century Britain
24. Twentieth-Century Britain
25. Heidegger
26. Ancient Philosophy
27. Socrates
28. Marx
29. Logic
30. Descartes
31. Machiavelli
32. Aristotle
33. Hume
34. Nietzsche
35. Darwin
36. The European Union
37. Gandhi
38. Augustine
39. Intelligence
40. Jung
41. Buddha
42. Paul
43. Continental Philosophy
44. Galileo
45. Freud
46. Wittgenstein
47. Indian Philosophy
48. Rousseau
49. Hegel
50. Kant
51. Cosmology
52. Drugs
53. Russian Literature
54. The French Revolution
55. Philosophy
56. Barthes
57. Animal Rights
58. Kierkegaard
59. Russell
60. William Shakespeare
61. Clausewitz
62. Schopenhauer
63. The Russian Revolution
64. Hobbes
65. World Music
66. Mathematics
67. Philosophy of Science
68. Cryptography
69. Quantum Theory
70. Spinoza
71. Choice Theory
72. Architecture
73. Poststructuralism
74. Postmodernism
75. Democracy
76. Empire
77. Fascism
78. Terrorism
79. Plato

80. Ethics
81. Emotion
82. Northern Ireland
83. Art Theory
84. Locke
85. Modern Ireland
86. Globalization
87. The Cold War
88. The History of Astronomy
89. Schizophrenia
90. The Earth
91. Engels
92. British Politics
93. Linguistics
94. The Celts
95. Ideology
96. Prehistory
97. Political Philosophy
98. Postcolonialism
99. Atheism
100. Evolution
101. Molecules
102. Art History
103. Presocratic Philosophy
104. The Elements
105. Dada and Surrealism
106. Egyptian Myth
107. Christian Art
108. Capitalism
109. Particle Physics
110. Free Will
111. Myth
112. Ancient Egypt
113. Hieroglyphs
114. Medical Ethics
115. Kafka
116. Anarchism
117. Ancient Warfare
118. Global Warming
119. Christianity
120. Modern Art
121. Consciousness
122. Foucault
123. The Spanish Civil War
124. The Marquis de Sade
125. Habermas
126. Socialism
127. Dreaming
128. Dinosaurs
129. Renaissance Art
130. Buddhist Ethics
131. Tragedy
132. Sikhism
133. The History of Time
134. Nationalism
135. The World Trade
      Organization
136. Design
137. The Vikings
138. Fossils
139. Journalism
140. The Crusades
141. Feminism
142. Human Evolution
143. The Dead Sea Scrolls
144. The Brain
145. Global Catastrophes
146. Contemporary Art
147. Philosophy of Law
148. The Renaissance
149. Anglicanism
150. The Roman Empire
151. Photography
152. Psychiatry
153. Existentialism
154. The First World War
155. Fundamentalism
156. Economics
157. International Migration
158. Newton
159. Chaos
160. African History
161. Racism
162. Kabbalah
163. Human Rights
164. International Relations
165. The American Presidency
166. The Great Depression and
      The New Deal
167. Classical Mythology

168. The New Testament as Literature
169. American Political Parties and Elections
170. Bestsellers
171. Geopolitics
172. Antisemitism
173. Game Theory
174. HIV/AIDS
175. Documentary Film
176. Modern China
177. The Quakers
178. German Literature
179. Nuclear Weapons
180. Law
181. The Old Testament
182. Galaxies
183. Mormonism
184. Religion in America
185. Geography
186. The Meaning of Life
187. Sexuality
188. Nelson Mandela
189. Science and Religion
190. Relativity
191. The History of Medicine
192. Citizenship
193. The History of Life
194. Memory
195. Autism
196. Statistics
197. Scotland
198. Catholicism
199. The United Nations
200. Free Speech
201. The Apocryphal Gospels
202. Modern Japan
203. Lincoln
204. Superconductivity
205. Nothing
206. Biography
207. The Soviet Union
208. Writing and Script
209. Communism
210. Fashion
211. Forensic Science
212. Puritanism
213. The Reformation
214. Thomas Aquinas
215. Deserts
216. The Norman Conquest
217. Biblical Archaeology
218. The Reagan Revolution
219. The Book of Mormon
220. Islamic History
221. Privacy
222. Neoliberalism
223. Progressivism
224. Epidemiology
225. Information
226. The Laws of Thermodynamics
227. Innovation
228. Witchcraft
229. The New Testament
230. French Literature
231. Film Music
232. Druids
233. German Philosophy
234. Advertising
235. Forensic Psychology
236. Modernism
237. Leadership
238. Christian Ethics
239. Tocqueville
240. Landscapes and Geomorphology
241. Spanish Literature
242. Diplomacy
243. North American Indians
244. The U.S. Congress
245. Romanticism
246. Utopianism
247. The Blues
248. Keynes
249. English Literature
250. Agnosticism
251. Aristocracy
252. Martin Luther
253. Michael Faraday

254. Planets
255. Pentecostalism
256. Humanism
257. Folk Music
258. Late Antiquity
259. Genius
260. Numbers
261. Muhammad
262. Beauty
263. Critical Theory
264. Organizations
265. Early Music
266. The Scientific Revolution
267. Cancer
268. Nuclear Power
269. Paganism
270. Risk
271. Science Fiction
272. Herodotus
273. Conscience
274. American Immigration
275. Jesus
276. Viruses
277. Protestantism
278. Derrida
279. Madness
280. Developmental Biology
281. Dictionaries
282. Global Economic History
283. Multiculturalism
284. Environmental Economics
285. The Cell
286. Ancient Greece
287. Angels
288. Children's Literature
289. The Periodic Table
290. Modern France
291. Reality
292. The Computer
293. The Animal Kingdom
294. Colonial Latin American Literature
295. Sleep
296. The Aztecs
297. The Cultural Revolution
298. Modern Latin American Literature
299. Magic
300. Film
301. The Conquistadors
302. Chinese Literature
303. Stem Cells
304. Italian Literature
305. The History of Mathematics
306. The U.S. Supreme Court
307. Plague
308. Russian History
309. Engineering
310. Probability
311. Rivers
312. Plants
313. Anaesthesia
314. The Mongols
315. The Devil
316. Objectivity
317. Magnetism
318. Anxiety
319. Australia
320. Languages
321. Magna Carta
322. Stars
323. The Antarctic
324. Radioactivity
325. Trust
326. Metaphysics
327. The Roman Republic
328. Borders
329. The Gothic
330. Robotics
331. Civil Engineering
332. The Orchestra
333. Governance
334. American History
335. Networks
336. Spirituality
337. Work
338. Martyrdom
339. Colonial America
340. Rastafari
341. Comedy

342. The Avant-Garde
343. Thought
344. The Napoleonic Wars
345. Medical Law
346. Rhetoric
347. Education
348. Mao
349. The British Constitution
350. American Politics
351. The Silk Road
352. Bacteria
353. Symmetry
354. Marine Biology
355. The British Empire
356. The Trojan War
357. Malthus
358. Climate
359. The Palestinian-Israeli Conflict
360. Happiness
361. Diaspora
362. Contemporary Fiction
363. Modern War
364. The Beats
365. Sociolinguistics
366. Food
367. Fractals
368. Management
369. International Security
370. Astrobiology
371. Causation
372. Entrepreneurship
373. Tibetan Buddhism
374. The Ancient Near East
375. American Legal History
376. Ethnomusicology
377. African Religions
378. Humour
379. Family Law
380. The Ice Age
381. Revolutions
382. Classical Literature
383. Accounting
384. Teeth
385. Physical Chemistry
386. Microeconomics
387. Landscape Architecture
388. The Eye
389. The Etruscans
390. Nutrition
391. Coral Reefs
392. Complexity
393. Alexander the Great
394. Hormones
395. Confucianism
396. American Slavery
397. African American Religion
398. God
399. Genes
400. Knowledge
401. Structural Engineering
402. Theatre
403. Ancient Egyptian Art and Architecture
404. The Middle Ages
405. Materials
406. Minerals
407. Peace
408. Iran
409. World War II
410. Child Psychology
411. Sport
412. Exploration
413. Microbiology
414. Corporate Social Responsibility
415. Love
416. Psychotherapy
417. Chemistry
418. Human Anatomy
419. The American West
420. American Political History
421. Ritual
422. American Women's History
423. Dante
424. Ancient Assyria
425. Plate Tectonics
426. Corruption
427. Pilgrimage
428. Taxation

ONLINE CATALOGUE
A Very Short Introduction

Our online catalogue is designed to make it easy to find your ideal Very Short Introduction. View the entire collection by subject area, watch author videos, read sample chapters, and download reading guides.

http://fds.oup.com/www.oup.co.uk/general/vsi/index.html

SOCIAL MEDIA
Very Short Introduction

Join our community

www.oup.com/vsi

- Join us online at the official Very Short Introductions **Facebook** page.
- Access the thoughts and musings of our authors with our online **blog**.
- Sign up for our monthly **e-newsletter** to receive information on all new titles publishing that month.
- Browse the full range of Very Short Introductions online.
- Read **extracts** from the Introductions for free.
- Visit our library of **Reading Guides**. These guides, written by our expert authors will help you to question again, why you think what you think.
- If you are a teacher or lecturer you can order inspection copies quickly and simply via our website.